The Special Educator and Job Stress

The Authors

Charles V. L. Dedrick is Professor of Educational Psychology, University of Northern Iowa, Cedar Falls.

Donna B. Raschke is Coordinator for Learning Disabilities and Early Childhood Special Education, and Associate Professor, Department of Special Education, University of Northern Iowa, Cedar Falls.

The Advisory Panel

Miryam Bujanda, EMT Instructor, Research Associate/Emergency Medical Technology Program, El Paso Community College, Texas

Anne M. Cancelmo, Learning Disabilities Teacher/Consultant, Mainland Regional High School, Linwood, New Jersey

Glenna Clark, New Directions Teacher, Special Education Department, New Canaan, Connecticut

Robert J. Evans, Associate Professor of Special Education, Co-Direcor, Marshall University Reading and Learning Center, Marshall University, Huntington, West Virginia

John T. Finnegan, Diagnostic Prescriptive Resource Teacher, Department of Special Services, Westerly School Department, Rhode Island

Thomas McKibben, Special Education Teacher, Ashford High School, Alabama

Lora Mehrer, Special Educator, Missoula, Montana

Nadine Sieber, Learning Disabilities Teacher, P. A. Tipler Middle School, Oshkosh, Wisconsin

The Special Educator and Job Stress

Charles V. L. Dedrick
and Donna B. Raschke

nea PROFESSIONAL LIBRARY
National Education Association
Washington, D.C.

Authors' Acknowledgments

I want to thank two special people for their unending support and encouragement during the writing of this book—my husband, James Rutherford Peterson, for his feedback, care, concern, and the many times he kept young Jennifer busy so I could write. Without his support, this book would be only an ideal and not a reality. I also wish to thank my daughter Jennifer for her continual zest and enthusiasm for living. Her invigorating spirit kept me going even when the sky was gray. You two, Jim and Jennifer, clearly enabled me to be all that I can be and greatly facilitated the production of this manuscript.

—Donna B. Raschke

I wish to express many thanks to Phyllis, my wife, who read and critiqued the entire manuscript, and whose experiences as a special educator provided much food for thought. I also wish to thank Deborah, Scott, and Brian, who allowed their father to write on weekends without experiencing undue guilt. Lastly, I wish to thank our typist, Marilyn Busch, whose expediency and thoroughness are dependable trademarks, and our secretary, Carol Aswegan, who made numerous trips to the fax machine.

—Charles V. L. Dedrick

Printing History
   First Printing: April 1990

Note

The opinions expressed in this publication should not be construed as representing the policy or position of the National Education Association. Materials published by the NEA Professional Library are intended to be discussion documents for teachers who are concerned with specialized interests of the profession.

Library of Congress Cataloging-in-Publication Data

Dedrick, Charles V. L.
    The special educator and job stress / Charles V. L. Dedrick and
Donna B. Raschke.
        p.   cm. — (NEA aspects of learning)
    Includes bibliographical references.
    ISBN 0-8106-3005-2
    1. Special education teachers—Job stress.   2. Burn out
(Psychology)   I. Raschke, Donna Bright, 1946-   . II. Title.
III. Series.
    LB2840.2.D43   1990
    371.9'01'9—dc20

                                                    89-78387
                                                    CIP

CONTENTS

PREFACE

You've had it, you say! Simply getting up in the morning and dragging yourself to school is pure agony. The demands of the profession just seem too great. Yes, you wanted to help children with special needs and you genuinely felt you had the patience and determination to work with these students with varying problems and limited capabilities. But no one told you it was going to be like this.

You know very well what it is like. You're there every day in the trenches, so to speak, coping with the demands that accompany teaching students with diverse needs. It's a challenge, indeed, and daily you face:

1. *Students* who are consistently unpredictable in their behavior, erratic in their performance, and who don't learn things in ways you and I do

2. *Parents* who are frustrated, angry at the system and, perhaps, at the end of their rope themselves as they watch their child struggle to master even the simplest task

3. *Regular educators* who are jealous of the fact that special educators work with only eight students and who are often reluctant to cooperate when a meeting is scheduled to consider the possibility of mainstreaming a student into their classroom, even if it is for only a half hour a day, three times a week

4. *Professional support staff* who are always too busy, overbooked, and unavailable, and seem more interested in identifying and classifying students rather than in identifying the most appropriate pedagogical practices

5. *Administrators* who would prefer to have these disruptive students assigned to another school.

Unfortunately, as many special educators note, these stressful conditions in the workplace are just the tip of the iceberg. Individualized educational plans, interdisciplinary team meetings, and constant demands to restructure and tailor educational materials to meet the needs of students who are often underachieving and overdemanding are ever-present realities. Clearly, no one informed you, adequately prepared you, or even hinted to you that it was going to be like this. Working with special-needs students, and with parents, regular educators, professional support staff, and administrators to design and deliver an appropriate educational program is, indeed, a major challenge.

Unequivocally, special education teachers face daily demands and requirements that regular education teachers do not. This monograph examines stressors encountered by special educators, ways of coping with professional demands, and reasons why some teachers handle job stress better than others. It is intended to help special education teachers take a more objective look at what they do and identify for themselves strategies and techniques to alleviate some of the stress and tension they encounter in the classroom. So come out of the trenches, make yourself comfortable, and see if any of the scenarios described seem hauntingly familiar. Most importantly, take an objective look at how you are dealing with the stress and tensions that evolve from working with special-needs students. The challenge is yours. And the fact that you have picked up this monograph indicates your commitment to a happier, healthier you.

1. STRESS AND BURNOUT

PROFILE OF A BURNED-OUT TEACHER: A TYPICAL SCENARIO

Becky has been teaching students with a variety of handicapping conditions in a resource room in a large urban high school for the past 10 years. Each class period she works with three or four students, all of whom have serious learning difficulties. All of her students have difficulty in abstracting meaning from the printed word, a problem that also results in writing and speaking deficiencies. Some of her students have low impulse control, which has, at times, resulted in expulsion and/or assignment to residential treatment facilities specializing in explosive, antisocial behavior. An analysis of the home life of Becky's students reveals frequent incidences of abuse and neglect. In addition, a few of the students display borderline abilities in verbal and performance scores on standardized intelligence tests.

Becky started her teaching career with a high degree of commitment and expectation. As her career progressed, she had good days and bad days. When her students made academic and social gains, she derived great personal satisfaction. In the past two years, however, Becky has been much less sensitive to her students' myriad needs, has become argumentative at staffings, and has found conferences with parents to be stressful and frustrating. She often leaves work tired and irritated, and she has used the maximum number of sick leave days allotted because of a constant nagging backache. Over the last two years, she has had to resort to a variety of over-the-counter medications. This once genuinely committed educator no longer enjoys the daily interactions with students and has begun to think seriously about a career change. In short, Becky exemplifies the profile of a burned-out teacher.

INTRODUCTION

The concept of burnout has its historical roots in the pioneering works of researchers such as Herbert Freudenberger, Christina Maslach, and Ayale Pines. For example, Maslach (1)* was interested in what happened to people who had intense personal encounters with others—i.e., professionals who deal on a daily basis with individuals manifesting psychologi-

---

*Numbers in parentheses appearing in the text refer to the References beginning on page 82.

cal, social, and physical problems. She found that some people could not cope with these continual, intense interpersonal transactions. The result was often a professional who responded to clients in a detached, dehumanized manner. Maslach identified three core aspects of burnout: emotional exhaustion, depersonalization, and feelings of low accomplishment (2).

Burnout has been defined in a variety of ways. Some researchers feel that one of the major problems in understanding it is the lack of a common definition (3). In a generic sense, Blase described burnout as a catchall term broadly describing any negative response by a person to work-related stress (4). Briefly, then, a burned-out classroom teacher is an individual who is less sympathetic toward students, frequently feels emotionally or physically exhausted, and has a much lower tolerance for frustration (5).

Kaiser (6) developed an interesting model based on the writings of Herzberg and Maslow. Kaiser identified factors that prevent job dissatisfaction and differentiated them from those that lead to job satisfaction. Salary, fringe benefits, and working conditions prevent individuals from being unhappy with their jobs. But the higher-level needs for esteem and actualization are what lead to job satisfaction. Variables such as personal accomplishment, professional advancement, and job enrichment are the real intrinsic benefits of teaching. These are the deposits that enhance one's professional bank account.

To appreciate the relevance of these ideas for special educators, one must take a hard look at the reality of the workplace. To be sure, salary, medical benefits, and sufficient classroom space make a difference. These conditions prevent teachers from being dissatisfied. However, the intrinsic benefits of the profession come from the gains that students make personally, socially, and academically. As Schwab points out, teachers enter the profession not for high salaries but for the opportunity to help students (7). Thus, professional self-image is closely linked to the progress made by students (8). This is the case whether one is working with mentally handicapped, learning-disabled, or behaviorally disordered students. The real deflator of the professional dream is a composite of all those things that inhibit the realization of one's professional goals. Within this context, it is important to realize that special educators work with students who have impaired abilities; consequently the gains they observe might be relatively small compared to those of other student populations. Since a teacher's professional goals are inextricably associated with student growth, then, factors such as disruptive students, uncooperative parents, insensitive regular educators, and apathetic administrators all contribute to job stress.

DeShong raised an interesting point, suggesting that there might be a cultural attitude that attributes superhuman qualities to those who work with special-needs students (9). Perhaps some special educators internalize this attitude and experience guilt when they do not meet self-imposed expectations.

Many burned-out teachers resolve their feelings of frustration and disillusionment by leaving the profession. They simply come to a point in their professional journey when they can no longer muster the energy or commitment to continue. Another group of teachers, who also experience serious job-related stress but do not leave the profession, are commonly referred to as "rust outs." These teachers no longer have the fire or excitement running through their "teacher bones"; they are literally rusting out. They continue in the classroom but perform in a manner far below their ability.

A point of clarification should be made here. Many in the teaching profession experience transient stress such as the loss of a loved one, a midlife crisis, or a painful divorce. These are certainly periods of great distress, and it is a rare individual who can totally mask these feelings in the classroom. Nevertheless, in most cases the devastating trauma abates and the individual continues his/her service to student needs. In contrast, when we talk about teachers rusting out, we are identifying a chronic problem that haunts America's schools. One would hope that within the structure of education, there are remediatory and enrichment experiences (in-service workshops, support groups, etc.) that could help restore these teachers to a satisfactory level of job performance.

Accumulated evidence supports the fact that teacher burnout is a serious problem in the United States (10). The term has become a catchall phrase for stress-related problems that have resulted in an alarming exodus from the profession. Each year thousands of classroom educators leave the profession—some primarily for economic reasons, but many because they have found teaching to be unrewarding in light of public criticism, conflicting societal expectations, lack of support from parents and administrators, and students who no longer possess the attributes necessary for sustained academic learning (11). In fact, as a result of job-related stress, as many as 50 percent of educators have indicated a genuine interest in leaving the profession (12, 13, 14, 15, 16).

It is widely recognized that special educators are very much affected by the pressures that accompany working with children and youth who present a wide variety of societal and academic challenges (17). As Zabel, Boomer and King stated (18), special educators are often caught in a vicious cycle of unrealized expectations and negative experiences. In a related investigation, Olson and Matuskey reported that excessive paperwork, pupil-teacher relations, inadequate planning time, low salary, discipline of students, and student attitudes were primary sources of stress for special educators performing in a variety of service delivery system roles (19). And Greer and Wethered found that the heavy demands placed on special educators—due process hearings, placement team meetings, diagnostic testing requirements, and consulting—significantly contribute to stress (20). These authors emphasized that teachers often work in isolation from other adults; class schedules and student needs restrict interaction with peers. Indications are that stress reactions of special educators often result in interpersonal conflicts with other professionals (e.g., with regular and special educators, and administrators), resistance to change, and rapid staff turnover (21, 22).

Some less effective approaches used by special educators to deal with stress include providing less direct services to children, lowering expectations for students, taking drugs (liquor, pills), and resigning from the profession (23). Obviously, nonproductive approaches to dealing with job-related stress result in a sharp reduction in the quantity and quality of services provided to meet the needs of exceptional students. In a series of studies, the authors found that special educators in general employed many productive methods to reduce job stress and the vast majority reported they had not seriously considered leaving the profession (24). Plaudits go to these professionals who obviously enjoy the challenge of educating students who present a wide range of individual needs.

2. BEWARE: IT COULD HAPPEN TO YOU

SYMPTOMS OF BURNOUT

There are a multitude of symptoms depicting burnout in classroom teachers. Some are idiosyncratic, such as the teacher who no longer found pleasure in listening to her classical music collection after a hard day's work. She was too keyed up. In fact, she found that she no longer enjoyed any of her hobbies because she was unable to relax in her free time. Preoccupation with negative thoughts about one's profession is a blatant indicator of stress. Additionally, there are a variety of generic symptoms, either physiological or psychological in nature, that are clear indicators that stress overload is occurring. Insomnia, overeating/over-drinking, and headaches/backaches accompanied by feelings of immobilization, distress, and irritability are often described as key indicators of distress. Also, rigidity in thinking may occur as teachers lose their ability to generate options in problem solving. Many educators report that they bombard themselves all day long with thoughts of recent failures—e.g., lack of progress in IEP goals. As a result, personal worth becomes jeopardized due to feelings of professional incompetence and personal inadequacy. Teachers begin to question the fruits of their labors in terms of the time and energy invested in instructional activities.

Five basic characteristics are frequently cited as denoting burnout:

1. A variety of physical problems brought on by nervous system reaction
2. Detachment or distancing from students
3. Pressure in personal and professional life
4. Emotionally destructive feelings from being unable to cope with stress
5. Cynical, dehumanized view of students. (25)

These classic symptoms are generally recognized in the literature. Unfortunately, burned-out teachers become less effective on the job. Because of daily preoccupation with personal discomfort, they become less committed to the educational programs of students. Resistance to change, malingering in the hallway or lounge, and frequent complaining are often cited by administrators as behavior symptoms they frequently observe in burned-out teachers (26).

13

BURNOUT SELF-AWARENESS

Because clichés such as "burnt to a crisp" or "stressed to the maximum" began to permeate the profession in the early seventies, many special education teachers asked themselves, "Am I a victim?" "Have I contracted the phenomenon?" Certainly, all teachers experience stress to some degree on a daily basis. The pencil sharpener becomes jammed, an unannounced fire drill interrupts a favorite slide presentation, and the mailbox overflows with five "same-day memos" requiring immediate attention. No one needs to tell teachers when they have had a bad day. Burnout and stress affect all educators. But in a more specific sense, to what degree are educators currently experiencing burnout? The questionnaire that follows was designed to help special educators take a more objective look at their own behavioral patterns to determine the degree of burnout they are experiencing. The more yes responses, the greater the indication of a significant degree of tension.

ADDITIONAL STRESSORS IN SPECIAL EDUCATION

Children who exhibit a wide range of individual differences can present major challenges. Because each child manifests a number of idiosyncratic instructional and social needs, it is essential to provide individualized educational approaches. When a particular procedure does not work, the teacher must modify the instructional program and incorporate an alternative teaching technique. If the student still cannot master the task, then additional, alternative techniques must be implemented and tried until mastery occurs. This can be extremely time-consuming; it requires a very tenacious teacher who has the stamina to try, try, and try again. In short, most students in regular education classes tend to achieve. Special-needs students, on the other hand, will learn and progress only under very specified and well-defined learning conditions. Many of them, for example, find little meaning in a star at the top of a paper or a pat on the back. Each of these students is unique as a result of her/his conditioning history. Therefore, it becomes a major challenge to identify what motivates them and turns them on to academic learning. Table 2.1 identifies 10 uniquenesses found in special education in contrast to regular education.

In contrast to regular educators, special educators have additional pedagogical responsibilities that can augment job stress and diminish job satisfaction. Individualized educational plans, diagnostic assessment requirements, and multidisciplinary team meetings are frequently noted stress points for teachers dealing with exceptional students. Table 2.2 provides a list of 10 additional sources of stress that, encountered across time, can challenge even the most versatile, well-seasoned educator.

14

Self-Analysis/Stress-Awareness Questionnaire

Circle your answer to each question.

1. Have you changed schools or classrooms in the last two years because of dissatisfaction? Yes No

2. Does it seem as if you have been doing the same mundane activities for the last 10 years? Yes No

3. Do you find yourself blaming all the inappropriate behaviors exhibited by your students on parents and other teachers or variables outside your control? Yes No

4. Do you seldom find new challenges and areas in which you desire additional information each year? Yes No

5. Have you intermittently taken sick leave because you just could not face another day? Yes No

6. Do you find yourself assigning more of the direct instructional responsibilities to your associate teacher and assuming more of the clerical tasks yourself? Yes No

7. Do you find yourself dreading the return to school after a weekend and actually counting down the hours of "freedom" that remain? Yes No

8. Do you find yourself angry at your professional support staff because they are not sensitive to the rigorous demands of your job? Yes No

9. Do you find yourself routinely ordering films and filmstrips unrelated to instructional objectives to take up class time? Yes No

10. Do you feel as if you have been given a day of reprieve when a snow day is called and you do not have to face the troops? Yes No

11. Do you feel as if you work in the trenches and have lower status and prestige than the regular education teachers? Yes No

12. Are the successes of your students no longer the highlights of your day? Yes No

13. Do you find yourself frequently wishing you worked with a different categorical population in special education? Yes No

Self-Analysis/Stress-Awareness Questionnaire
(Continued)

14. Do you find yourself making if-only statements to rationalize low performance rates of your students throughout the day?   Yes   No

15. At the end of the day do you feel more like a tutor or babysitter than a teacher?   Yes   No

16. Do you find students behaving inappropriately more often than you find them behaving appropriately?   Yes   No

17. Do you complain to the administration regularly about the difficulties of working with special-needs students?   Yes   No

18. Do other professions look tremendously exciting and challenging in contrast to your boring, mundane routine?   Yes   No

Table 2.1
10 Uniquenesses Found in Special Education

1. Pupils who present a wider range of individual differences than those found in a regular classroom (27)

2. Pupils who frequently do not learn in ordinary traditional ways as their "normal"-peer counterparts do (28)

3. Pupils who look different from many of their "normal"-peer counterparts (29)

4. Pupils who come with lengthier histories of academic failure than their "normal"-peer counterparts (30)

5. Pupils who are less popular than their "normal"-peer counterparts (31)

6. Pupils who have fewer "people-pleasing behaviors" than their "normal"-peer counterparts (32)

7. Pupils who have fewer coping strategies when they encounter stress than their "normal"-peer counterparts (33)

8. Pupils who learn at a slower rate than their "normal"-peer counterparts (34)

9. Pupils who do not take as much responsibility for their successes and failures as their "normal"-peer counterparts do (35)

10. Pupils who do not provide as much reinforcement to themselves or to others as their "normal"-peer counterparts do (36)

Table 2.2
10 Additional Sources of Stress in Special Education
in Contrast to Regular Education

1. Individualized educational plans
2. Diagnostic testing requirements and consulting demands
3. Multidisciplinary team meetings
4. Due process hearings
5. Responsibilities to both regular and special education administrators
6. Parents who are struggling with lower expectations for their child
7. Isolation from other special educators
8. Class schedules with no breaks
9. Small, restricted work environments
10. Unpredictable students

STAGES AND CHARACTERISTICS OF BURNOUT

Many special educators are able to persevere effectively even under the most challenging conditions. They appear to possess a genetic stamina and tenacity that enables them to weather the storm. These educators are to be saluted and acknowledged for the fortitude to deal with professional demands across time. On the other hand, there are many special educators who do not possess this remarkable tenacity and who are in dire need of a tune-up.

The special education teachers who reach the burnout point are functioning far below their potential and generally suffer pain, stress, and frustration in teaching and extracurricular assignments. Such disenchantment with teaching can be plotted through four stages, which address the progression from an enthusiastic beginner to a disheartened rust out:

1. The Invigorated Good Shepherd
2. The Mundane, Repetitious Soldier
3. The Disgusted, Thwarted Rebel
4. The Apathetic, Unresponsive Robot

Generally these stages are hierarchical in nature; that is, they occur in logical, numerical order. Occasionally, however, a teacher may skip a stage and even regress to a previously helpless pattern of thinking. The time spent at

17

any particular stage reflects the degree of support both internal and external provided to the teacher. Familiarity with each stage can help educators know when it is time to take preventive action.

The Invigorated Good Shepherd

In this stage, special education teachers have just completed a training program and are full of idealism and grandiose visions of ways they can help students who traditionally have a history of failure. Often, novice teachers hold unrealistically high expectations about the major contributions they plan to make. With an abundance of energy these beginning practitioners are prime candidates for becoming workaholics. Many see themselves as solely responsible for the design and implementation of educational programs uniquely tailored to meet each student's needs. Not only do they attempt to modify curriculum to meet each student's characteristics, but they design elaborate behavioral management programs that are in reality appropriate only for laboratory settings where several behavioral engineers are available to record and tabulate all required data. For many of these educators, their work becomes the only important thing in their lives.

The Mundane, Repetitious Soldier

In this stage, special educators begin to question their idealism and lose their enthusiasm. Entering the classroom no longer brings a thrill, and feelings of dissatisfaction begin. The excitement over implementing a new behavior management program or developing a new social skill unit begins to dwindle. Feelings of isolation emerge as well as the awareness that personal effort is being expended without much appreciation. The special educator begins to note hostility from some regular educators and questions such as, "What do you do all day with only six youngsters?" become repetitious. While no openly hostile confrontation occurs, underlying feelings of isolation pervade the professional self. The initial thrill of being a special educator and dedicating one's life to helping others who have academic and behavioral deficits begins to fade. The stress of the job begins to take its toll physically and psychologically. Less time and effort are put into designing and implementing IEPs for each student, and concerns about such previously mundane issues as salary, working hours, and professional growth begin to emerge.

The Disgusted, Thwarted Rebel

In this stage, the special educator becomes bombarded by feelings of helplessness. No matter how great the effort, the teacher is unable to ef-

18

fect appreciable change in certain students' lives. One family refuses to attend conferences, another student arrives 30 to 60 minutes late each day, and there are an endless number of roadblocks in securing support services for several extremely needy students. In short, the reality of teaching special-needs students is *not* what was anticipated. Stress has developed to such an extent that special educators begin to question the value of their career choice as well as their own sense of professional competence. Statements such as "I really don't make any difference here anyway" are mumbled to oneself over and over. Other occupations start to look more attractive to many teachers at this point.

The Apathetic and Unresponsive Robot

In this stage, special educators are chronically frustrated and overwhelmed, yet they feel powerless to change anything significantly. As a result, they withdraw emotionally from painful situations and perform like robots who come to work, meet the minimal requirements of the job, and teach what has been taught previously regardless of the needs of students. They clearly believe they have no impact on effecting change in the behavior of students. In other words, they are apathetic and simply go through the motions of teaching.

It is important that special educators recognize where they are in the stress cycle so that they may face the challenge head-on and attempt to identify constructive strategies to alleviate the symptoms described. Table 2.3 addresses the major symptoms in each stage. If any of these sound familiar, we encourage you to take a constructive proactive approach in identifying and implementing procedures designed to reduce stress (see Chapter 6).

Table 2.3
Stages of Burnout

Below are several statements representative of each stage of the burn-out process. Answer each question as honestly as possible by circling yes or no. In which stage, if any, do most of your yes responses occur?

The Invigorated Good Shepherd

1. Did you recently complete a special education teacher training program? Yes No

2. Do you regularly work more than an eight-hour day? Yes No

3. Do you try to rely on your inner resources rather than utilize your support team to solve major problems? Yes No

4. Do you design elaborate behavior management or instructional programs tailored to each child's unique characteristics? Yes No

5. Do you feel you can be successful with every special-needs student with whom you are assigned to work? Yes No

The Mundane, Repetitious Soldier

1. Is your enthusiasm for teaching beginning to dwindle? Yes No

2. Do you have occasional headaches or other physical ailments reflecting a difficult day at work? Yes No

3. Do you feel isolated and believe that the majority of regular educators do not understand your role or mission? Yes No

4. Is teaching special-needs students a bit more mundane than you first thought? Yes No

5. Do you feel as if you are spending too much time on pedagogical matters and you should be spending more time with significant others in your life? Yes No

Table 2.3
Stages of Burnout
(Continued)

The Disgusted, Thwarted Rebel

1. Are your physical problems increasing in frequency or complexity?   Yes   No

2. Do there seem to be multiple obstacles that, no matter how hard you try, you cannot seem to overcome?   Yes   No

3. Do you question the value of teaching and wonder if you are really helping any of the special-needs students under your tutelage?   Yes   No

4. Do you find yourself frequently thinking things such as, "I don't really make a difference here anyway"?   Yes   No

5. Are other occupations starting to look more appealing to you than teaching?   Yes   No

The Apathetic, Unresponsive Robot

1. Are you completely exhausted at the end of the school day?   Yes   No

2. Do you use the same techniques and procedures over and over regardless of the needs of students?   Yes   No

3. Do you feel like a robot simply going through daily routines with a mechanical orientation?   Yes   No

4. Do you feel completely powerless to significantly change things?   Yes   No

5. Do you dislike teaching, but just see too many obstacles for making a career change at this point in your life?   Yes   No

3. THE IMPACT OF STRESS ON TEACHERS, STUDENTS, AND ORGANIZATIONAL COMPONENTS

INTRODUCTION

As Hans Selye has pointed out (37), there are many different kinds of stress in the everyday world. Indeed, stress is inevitable. And, some degree of stress is necessary for individuals to mobilize; that is, an appropriate amount of anxiety, which will differ from person to person, galvanizes individuals to accept challenges and deal effectively with situations that are sometimes uncertain or discrepant. Deliberate avoidance of new and different situations can bring about a condition of stagnation and sterility. Positive anxiety, often called eustress, is the stuff that individual growth is made of. When individuals feel that a situation or event is within their range of capability, but not achievable without a certain degree of effort, they face "challenge." On the other hand, perceptions of threat bring about anticipations of failure. Distress is bad stress, a situation or event that forces the human system to make quick adaptations that often wreak havoc on one's psychological and physical well-being.

It is also important to realize that individuals differ in their ability to handle stressful events. For a variety of reasons (some hereditary, some environmental), one individual can muster the necessary resources to overcome trauma, while another, in a similar situation, will become incapacitated. Individuals also differ in terms of their optimal tempo or pace of life. Some, like racehorses, seem to be constantly on the go and indeed almost welcome change and dissonance. Others, like turtles, move along at a slower pace and seem content to approach life in a much more calm, reflective manner (38).

THE IMPACT OF STRESS ON TEACHERS

We have previously discussed the symptoms of teacher burnout especially as they apply to special educators, delineating the impact of stress on the physical, emotional, and psychological well-being of the individual teacher. We would now like to focus on the manner in which job stress affects professional performance, particularly in relation to students with exceptional needs. Most research on teacher burnout focuses on the fact that when helping professionals feel distressed, they begin to dis-

22

tance themselves from their clients or students. This was the condition of Becky in our opening scenario (see p. 9). Along with this depersonalization comes a lowered tolerance for frustrating events; in short, the teacher becomes quick to anger when students do not behave in appropriate ways. In matters of discipline there is a greater probability that a teacher experiencing job stress will resort to punitive measures to keep students on task. These might include yelling at students, excessive time-out, and the occasional use of corporal punishment. The classroom situation of the burned-out teacher is often one that is out of control. A burned-out teacher is more than likely preoccupied with a set of pressing personal concerns and is much less sensitive to factors that either add to or take away from a student's self-worth. In addition, the teacher's inability to concentrate and focus on instructional tasks results in a learning environment that is often disorganized and lacks coherence. Burned-out teachers are often all-consumed with efforts to survive, to just get through the day. The teacher who is distraught and finds students and their accompanying academic and social needs to be a source of dissatisfaction is likely to cast a negative shadow over the entire school community. Therefore, the teacher who is undergoing a chronic condition of job dissatisfaction does not usually deteriorate in a vacuum. He or she strikes out, depriving students of good educational experiences, jeopardizing relationships with other staff members, and portraying a picture of incompetence to parents and the school community.

THE IMPACT OF STRESS ON STUDENTS

The issue of teacher burnout becomes critical when one considers the student populations served by special educators—students with emotional problems, students with learning difficulties, students who are mentally deficient, and students who have attentional deficits. The fact that these students present a number of academic and social disabilities exacerbates the condition of poor teaching. They may be more vulnerable, more devastated by poor teaching than "regular" students. Their disabilities make it more difficult for them to rebound from a distressed teacher. Their deficits become greater, their coping skills less adequate, and their self-worth is seriously jeopardized.

As we have previously emphasized, many students with exceptional needs are at risk to begin with. Epanchin and Paul have pointed out that behaviorally disordered (BD) students in particular are more adversely affected by a teacher's negative reaction than are other special-needs students (39). When social and academic problems are compounded, special education students are hard pressed to respond with effective coping strategies. These students are different from regular students in a num-

23

ber of ways; many of these differences are delineated in Table 2.1.

It is also important to remember that special education students often have instructional arrangements that are different from those of other students. Some spend an entire day with one teacher (and perhaps a teacher assistant) in a self-contained classroom setting; others visit a resource room one period a day; still others work in a self-contained-with-integrated situation. Another important fact to remember is that in most cases the teacher-pupil ratio is relatively low. This is an asset when a good teacher develops effective educational programs for each student. However, it becomes a liability when a small number of students are in direct proximity to a burned-out, highly stressed teacher. The following section describes what can happen to special education students in such a situation.

The Effects on Students

One unproductive strategy students might employ to relieve a high-anxiety situation is to withdraw. They may begin to daydream excessively in an effort to escape a teacher who is verbally abusive or consistently negative. They may appear to give surface submission to a tyrannical teacher, but in large measure they have begun to shut down in an effort to distance themselves from aversive stimuli. Another tactic would be to engage in a work stoppage—that is, to passively resist any effort exerted by the teacher to engage them in compliant behaviors. A third withdrawal response would be to become completely indifferent to what is happening in the classroom. In short, students may simply stop processing information. The withdrawal response on the part of special education students is doubly dangerous. First of all, some exceptional students are socially withdrawn to begin with and very apprehensive in social and academic settings. An oppressive teacher may cause them to withdraw even further into a shell of silence and unresponsiveness. Then, too, when students are deliberately engaging in escapist tactics, they are not learning. In essence, they are employing defensive postures that literally cut them off from the very instruction and individualized programs that have been designed to remediate their deficiencies. For the student, this is a no-win situation.

A second unproductive strategy would be to engage in countercontrol measures—that is, to attack the source of frustration and anguish. When a teacher is especially punitive and clearly disinterested in student needs, the class members (individually or collectively) may begin to plan strategies to undermine the teacher's efforts. This results in a potentially explosive situation, often similar to open warfare. Such a strategy would certainly heighten the problems of students who are diagnosed as emotionally disturbed. A corollary of this strategy is the ripple effect (40). One student engages in an inappropriate behavior and subsequently all the others begin to follow suit. Examples of this type of contagious behavior include pencil tapping, foot stomping, or engaging in a high degree of verbal interaction.

Other techniques that might be employed by students who are experiencing stress are to lie, hide feelings, tattle on others, and regress. In all the instances previously described, students are attempting (either individually or as a group) to rid themselves of a highly unpleasant situation. And when students are busy trying to deal with high stress factors in their class environment, they are obviously much less likely to profit from any instructional activities.

When special education students are taught by burned-out teachers, their self-worth plummets dramatically. They fall farther behind academically and socially, and engage in unproductive compensatory behaviors out of desperation. They pay a dear price for an intolerable state of affairs. In a real sense, they have been denied the opportunity to grow and prosper to their fullest extent. They may be permanently scarred.

THE IMPACT OF STRESS ON ORGANIZATIONS

The authors have conducted a number of in-service workshops in various school districts. We have both commented on how it is often possible for a visitor to a school building to pick up vibrations that serve as rough approximations of school climate. School climate might be defined as a composite of the school culture, including norms, expectations, rituals, and symbols (41). To get a really good sense of what goes on in a school building, one would have to be immersed for several weeks in a rather intense field study using the tools of ethnographic research. To be certain, school climate does include an assessment of all the interlocking parts, students and staff alike. Matters such as morale and cohesiveness play a big part in the emotional tone that permeates a school building. In this sense, staff members who are locked into a burnout cycle can cause considerable harm with respect to organizational climate. The following are profiles of three highly stressed individuals and their impact on school climate.

The House Cynic

This person emanates negativism, using staffings, lunchrooms, and faculty meetings as forums to belittle students, criticize other staff members, and downgrade administration. It is as if, from the comic strip "'Lil Abner," a dark cloud accompanies her/him at all times. Unfortunately, these burned out teachers infect everyone else with their constant distress calls. In addition, they vent their anger and frustration on other staff members, literally using them for purposes of displaced aggression. Idealistically, one might like to confront these cynics, point our their flagrant negativism and find some mechanism in the system to provide remediation. Realistically, however, most staff members isolate themselves from these teachers in the best interests of their own professional survival. The major point is that house cynics dig deep into the culture of a school and take away from other staff members' sense of job satisfaction.

A.W.O.L.—Absent from Work

Another individual who is at risk with regard to job distress is the staff member who is frequently absent from work. One consequence of burnout is withdrawal, to spend as little time at the workplace as possible. These absentees are the ones who truly abuse sick leave policies. Sometimes they are really sick (whether psychosomatic or not); at other times, they simply do not want to come to work. Their frequent absences have a deleterious effect on the organizational climate. This is especially the case in special education where staffings and teamings are essential for the well-being of exceptional-needs children. Often meetings have to be canceled, IEPs put on hold, and late paperwork accumulates. Everyone pays the price in this scenario. Other staff members often have to take up the absentee's slack, putting additional burdens on their own already busy schedules. Services for exceptional-needs students, which put a high price on cooperation and coordination, are placed in jeopardy. Since there are no distinct rewards for excellence or penalties for incompetence, the morale of staff members is sorely strained by the frequent absences of burned-out teachers.

The Alfred E. Newman Syndrome—What, Me Worry?

The last group of individuals who cast a negative shadow on school culture are the foot-draggers, those who have become rigid and increasingly inflexible. They have lost the spark and enthusiasm that once made them good special education professionals. They approach their jobs with some measure of disdain, and are resistant to change and efforts at school improvement. They distrust new ideas and often actively sabotage efforts to introduce innovative programs. They see in-service workshops as time-wasters and are the last to arrive in the morning and the first to leave in the afternoon. Their apathy is a weight or a millstone for other staff members who must work closely with them. They frustrate the good intentions of colleagues and make deep inroads into staff morale.

26

The troublesome thing about all three of these scenarios is that it is difficult to remediate, or rejuvenate, or, in some cases, to remove these individuals from their present teaching assignments. These apathetic teachers are an ever-present source of discontent for other staff members.

THE NEED FOR INTERVENTION

Several strategies can be employed to reduce individual and organizational stress. The discussion that follows is limited to intervention programs that can be utilized as a school staff.

Letting Off Steam

It might be healthy to set aside weekly or bimonthly meetings in which all staff, regular and special educators, can have the opportunity to frankly express concerns about a number of issues of mutual interest. For example, there is often a tug of war between the goals of the organization and the goals of the individual. Open forums can bring about a greater sense of ownership and self-determination. In short, when teachers have a chance to talk about their difficulties, things do not seem so hopeless. The initiative for such meetings may have to come from the building administrator but it is possible that a critical mass of teachers could make the necessary arrangements. A word of caution: Although these meetings may be a good chance for catharsis, it is important that they be constructive, avoiding personal vendettas. Thus, ground rules should be established. Obviously, the chemistry of the mix of people attending the meetings makes a big difference. It might be a good idea to designate a secretary to take a narrative of the discussions. These notes can then become an agenda for followup meetings to develop a plan of action. This is especially important when there are distinct differences of opinion between regular and special educators regarding integrating exceptional students into regular classes.

Peer Mentoring

Both authors are consultants to an exchange program involving three school districts that has as its primary focus the mentoring of beginning teachers. According to the agreement, a new teacher in District X can be engaged in a mentoring exchange with an experienced teacher in District Y. We also see great benefit accruing from peer exchanges that would link master teachers with teachers who may be in the process of rusting out. It is believed that such an arrangement would be a good opportunity for an exchange of skills, which may be just the experience that rejuvenates the teacher going through a period of professional malaise. Interaction among staff members can provide teachers with critical information that they can use to enhance their sense of job efficacy (42). Given this context, there would seem to be many opportunities for rich exchanges between regular and special educators. If there is a strong possibility in the near future that regular and special educators will be working as a team, this preliminary exchange of insights and observations would be of great value. Although the main thrust of the peer exchange program is to fine tune instructional skills, one can clearly see many opportunities for peer collaboration.

Conflict Resolution

Interactions among individuals with different goals, backgrounds, and motivations will periodically involve differences and conflict. Clearly, regular and special educators approach the educational arena with somewhat different goals, backgrounds, and motivations. It is important for teachers to remember that relationships totally free of conflict may also be void of effective communication. When differences in mission and purpose do evolve between the regular and special educator, an analysis of potential causes can be useful. For example, ask yourself, Did the conflict evolve because of—

- a lack of common terms and jargon to accurately describe the situation?
- a lack of opportunity to exchange information on an ongoing basis?
- an absence of trust and acceptance of value differences?

Thomas Gordon in 1974 introduced the no-lose method of conflict resolution in his book *Teacher Effectiveness Training* (43). This method reduces resentment concerning a conflict resolution by encouraging individuals who own a mutual problem to go through a series of collaborative steps to arrive at an outcome both parties can live with. There is also a provision for implementing a specific plan of action as well as a follow-up evaluation.

Some situations may be classified as disastrous and in serious need of attention. Others may simply be brushfires, that left alone will burn themselves out. Situations perceived as having significant importance to both educators are, of course, more intricate and difficult to resolve. When extreme positions are taken with emotions raging, conflict resolutions can take on a win/lose flavor, creating an atmosphere that is not productive and should be avoided.

The principles of conflict resolution are based on four basic elements:

1. *People.* We are all people first. We bring our whole selves to any situation. It is important to focus on substance rather than relation-

ships. Relationships often become tangled on problems. Separate the people from the problem.

2. *Interests.* Interests define the problem. They motivate people. Your position is what you have decided upon. Your interests are what caused you to decide. For every interest there are several possible positions. Focus on interests—not positions.

3. *Options.* There is an abundance of possible solutions to solve any dilemma. A variety of options should be generated and the pros and cons of each solution delineated. The option that provides an equal balance of ''gives'' and ''takes'' for each party should be selected.

4. *Criteria.* Work toward using objective criteria in making agreements. Don't yield to pressure, only principle. Insist that the result be based on objective criteria.

Common resolution to conflict involves successive taking and then giving up a sequence of positions. Ultimately the conflict is resolved and agreements made. These agreements should—

- meet the legitimate interests of both sides
- resolve conflicting interests fairly
- be workable
- take common interests into account.

Special educators constantly ''negotiate'' with regular educators regarding the skills and behaviors students with special needs must exhibit if they are to be permitted to stay in the regular classroom. It is the special educator who must constantly ''bite the tongue'' and maintain composure when the expectations and demands of the regular educator appear blatantly unfair. Following are stock phrases many special educators have used when they feel their best intentions are thwarted or their well-meaning plans sabotaged by regular educators:

- Please correct me if I'm wrong . . .
- I appreciate what you've done for Johnny . . .
- My concern is fairness.
- Let me get back to you.
- One fair solution might be . . .
- Let me show you where I have difficulty following your ideas.

It is in the best interest of students with special needs for the special educator to be well versed in conflict resolution strategies. However, cooperation of the regular educator is essential if students are to be successfully mainstreamed. It is the experienced, committed teacher who has the stamina and tenacity to negotiate and renegotiate what it will take for a student to succeed in the least restrictive environment. There are strategies that can be used when conflicts arise between regular and special educators—strategies that can successfully resolve differences and maximize educational opportunities for special-needs students.

In-Service Workshops

In-service workshops attended by regular and special educators can provide many opportunities for a better understanding of the intent of PL 94–142 as well as the characteristics of special-needs students. It might be advisable to have a faculty committee plan and organize such workshops. This format increases involvement and faculty decision making. For example, in-service training programs might address strategies and techniques special educators can implement to alleviate stressors they will inevitably encounter. Information addressing techniques such as diet and exercise, relaxation techniques, social support systems, goal setting, time management, networking, compartmentalization of job and personal life, self-talk, GMSs (Good-to-Myselfs) and catching students being good (44) are described in the literature as proactive, constructive ways to overcome the ill effects of job-related stress. School systems are also encouraged to offer wellness programs utilizing stress-reduction techniques such as those listed above.

Additionally, in-service training for administrative personnel and regular educators is warranted based on special educators' frequent requests for staff collaboration. Particular attention should be devoted to providing information about easily implemented environmental adaptations and viable curriculum alterations for students who require highly structured educational programs to learn. Attention should also be given to ways that regular educators can organize and structure the educational environment to better accommodate students with diverse learning characteristics. These would include such strategies as cooperative learning, peer tutoring arrangements, and group reward contingencies. Of course, the benefits to be accrued when both regular and special-needs students work and learn together side by side should be emphasized (45, 46).

4. STRESS AND THE SPECIAL EDUCATOR

INTRODUCTION

Special educators work with students who present a number of social, physical, and academic challenges. Each child is unique, and with this exceptionality comes the need for an individualized program. For those preparing for a career in special education, a number of options are available with respect to student populations (i.e., learning-disabled students, behaviorally disordered students). It is also important to note that each state department of education may have a somewhat different set of certification requirements to qualify individuals for working with specific student populations. Consequently, the varying state requirements can restrict the special educator's freedom to relocate. In other words, educators may find that while they fully qualify to teach a particular categorical area in one state, they may not meet the certification standards in the same area in another state. Thus, mobility for relocating is much more restricted for special educators than it is for their colleagues in regular education.

Undergraduate students prepare for a career in special education by meeting requirements through a system of endorsements. Students can obtain certification in a variety of areas, including early childhood special education, severe and profoundly handicapped, learning disabled, behaviorally disordered, and mentally handicapped. This chapter focuses on the job stress of special educators certified in the last three areas—that is, teachers of students who are learning-disabled (LD), teachers of students with behavioral/emotional problems (BD), and teachers of students with mental deficiencies (MD).

First, however, we would like to review several studies that looked at job stress and the special educator from a generic, nonspecific perspective. The premise is that special educators as a group experience an array of job stressors that are different from those faced by regular educators as a group.

Schwab and Iwanicki discussed some of the major roles performed by special educators such as remediation of basic skills, modifying inappropriate behavior, and developing coping skills (47). In addition, special educators often must play such diverse roles as counselor, technician, curriculum specialist, record keeper, diagnostician, and expert in working with difficult students.

D'Alonzo and Wiseman reported that many special educators feel their professional roles are unclear or in conflict (48). This might be the case particularly when special educators are working within a regular school environment. As Zabel, Boomer, and King pointed out, the expectations a teacher has for job performance, which involve many of the roles discussed above, are the lens through which school experiences are perceived (49).

Rizzo, House, and Lirtzman distinguished between role conflict and role ambiguity (50). Role conflict is the occurrence of two or more sets of inconsistent role behaviors, while role ambiguity is the lack of clear information regarding one's duties and responsibilities. Both discrepancies in function have relevance for special educators. Inconsistency occurs when special educators play conflicting roles such as disciplinarian vs. therapist, or manager vs. innovator. In addition, special educators usually carry out their prescribed functions within a matrix of many support staff as well as regular educators. In this context, the building administrator plays a key role in making certain all staff members have a clear perception of role expectations.

Lawrenson and McKinnon found that the main reason some special educators resigned their position was hassles with administrators (51). In another study, surveying 365 full-time special education teachers, Fimian and Santoro found that many teachers felt that their personal priorities were being usurped by professional time demands (52). Additionally, the teachers in this sample felt that they did not receive enough recognition for the job they did; that promotion and advancement opportunities were minimal; that school disciplinary policies were inadequate; and that there was too little time for class preparation.

In another study, Bradfield and Fones found that special educators reported the greatest job stress in relationships with the parents of students (53). Other problem areas mentioned were time management, poor stress management techniques, unrealistic expectations for teacher performance, and inappropriate student behavior.

It is the contention of the authors that while there are many common denominators in pre-service special education preparation programs (such as behavior modification), there are also content areas and field experiences that are representative of each of the three areas. One could easily sketch three distinctive scenarios that would accurately represent the academic and social profiles of students who are labeled learning disabled, behaviorally disordered, and mentally disabled. This fact highlights the importance of preparing special educators who are well trained in behavioral and curricular matters specific to each student population. Additionally, while the workday of all special educators may have much in common, such as IEPs, the way that each professional deals with students involves a specific set of accommodations. The authors, then, make the assumption that while special educators may be seen collectively as professionals who work with exceptional students, there are considerable variations within the field, depending on the student population being served.

In 1984, the authors received a grant from the Iowa Department of Public Instruction to conduct a study with a two-pronged mission: (1) to identify major stressors in the professional lives of special educators; (2) to ascertain how special educators deal with stress in the workplace. The authors developed a survey instrument containing four elements: (a) a demographic page, (b) a rank ordering of 11 stressors previously identified by the literature, (c) a Q-sort adaptation asking respondents to sort 16 ways of dealing with stress, and (d) an open-ended section asking respondents to indicate the positive and negative aspects of what they do. The survey instrument was sent to a random sample of special educators working in LD, BD, and MD classrooms. The remainder of this chapter presents (1) the authors' data in each of the three categories, (2) a brief discussion of the results, (3) the findings of other studies conducted in each of the three areas, and (4) a conclusion in each area representative of the studies reviewed.

STRESSORS PECULIAR TO TEACHERS OF LEARNING-DISABLED STUDENTS

Scenario

John works with 18 students who have a variety of learning deficits. He spends a great deal of time preparing IEPs and diligently attempts to accommodate each student's unique disability. John feels he has been well prepared in terms of curricular programs and techniques of behavior management, but his main bone of contention is the attitude of the administration and of regular teachers. John's classroom is located across from the lunchroom in the basement of the school. He does not have space in the classroom for a full-sized traditional desk, and believes the placement of his room is indicative of his low priority on the school staff. He feels very isolated from regular class teachers. Sometimes he detects a note of annoyance from them when students are pulled out of regular classrooms to visit his resource room. He would like to develop a much closer working relationship with regular teachers with respect to curriculum and followup activities, but there seems to be resistance. He senses that other teachers resent the fact that he works with so few students. He rarely gets any positive feedback from the administration or other staff members about the hard work that he puts into providing appropriate learning environments for his students. Occasionally, John has to convince parents that the resource room experience is not a stigma, it does not mean that "his kids" are markedly different from other students. He firmly believes that the special environment of the resource room is beneficial to his students. John likes working with LD students; however, he feels frustrated by what he perceives as roadblocks to the fulfillment of his mission. He has a hard time getting resources and equipment for his program and he sometimes feels that other teachers see him as different. The isolation and lack of collegiality prohibit a full measure of job satisfaction.

The Data Base

A survey instrument was designed and disseminated to teachers of LD students to solicit the following information:

1. What are the major sources of stress impinging upon the professional lives of teachers of LD students?

2. What are the most desirable and undesirable aspects of the professional workplace of teachers of LD students?

This same survey instrument was also sent to teachers of BD and MD students, and thus is not discussed again in the next two sections. The number of respondents in each survey is represented in the tables.

Rank Order of Job-Related Stressors

An examination of the data in Table 4.1 indicates that the primary concern of teachers of LD students was the unmet needs of students with whom they work on a daily basis. A second area of job-related stress revolved around the necessity and complexity of writing IEPs, while the third most pressing source of stress was not having enough time to accomplish instructional tasks and related duties. Areas of lesser concern included isolation from colleagues, insufficient resources, and lengthy meetings. Relationships with regular educators, parents, and administrators were ranked in the middle group of stressors.

Desirable and Undesirable Aspects of the Profession

The research sample of teachers of LD students strongly identified working with students and observing their academic and social gains as the most enjoyable aspect of their job (Table 4.2). These teachers frequently mentioned the satisfaction they received when students began to acquire a repertoire of skills that allowed them to participate in the intrinsic joys of learning. These teachers also felt that the freedom to im-

34

Table 4.1
Rank Order of Stressors:
Teachers of LD Students
N = 79

1. Students' unmet needs
2. Paperwork (IEPs)
3. Lack of preparation time
4. Uncooperative students
5. Nonsupportive parents
6. Regular educators' attitudes
7. Large teacher-student ratio
8. Unhelpful administrators
9. Lack of support from specialized services
10. Lengthy meetings
11. Insufficient resources
12. Isolation from colleagues

plement curricular programs for students with special learning needs allowed them to control an important aspect of their daily work environment. Other job satisfiers identified were working in a collegial manner with selected teachers and support personnel, and the distinct advantage of working with small groups of students.

As suggested changes in the workplace, teachers of LD students emphasized the need for improved room accommodations, a better working relationship with regular education teachers, more planning time, and a concern that building administrators were neither knowledgeable nor helpful with respect to curricular and material requests in the area of special education.

Discussion of Survey Results

In assessing the data from the two major formats utilized by the survey instrument (rank ordering and open-ended questions), several recurring themes seem to represent substantive issues expressed by teachers of LD students in this sample.

A primary concern and major stressor identified by these teachers was the fact that many of the needs of learning-disabled students were not being met. Many of the teachers expressed frustration regarding their room accommodations. They complained that their rooms were too small (in one case the teacher was teaching in a closet); that they were situated

Table 4.2
Desirable and Undesirable Aspects of the Work
Environment: Teachers of LD Students
N = 79

	List three aspects of your job that you like				If you could change aspects of the environment in which you work, what would these changes be?		
Rank	Item	Frequency	Percent	Rank	Item	Frequency	Percent
1	Student progress	40	51%	1	Improve physical environment	35	44%
2	Freedom to implement	33	42%	2	More cooperation from regular teachers	26	33%
3	Interaction with students	30	38%	3	More planning time	17	22%
4	Interaction with colleagues	20	25%	4	More administrative support	13	16%
5	Small teacher-pupil ratio	15	19%				

in an environment in close proximity to a noisy and distracting cafeteria or band room; that there were no windows, and the room temperature was often difficult to control. In both the rank-ordering device and the open-ended questions, teachers of LD students complained about the lack of planning time, including time necessary to write extensive IEPs. These teachers felt that they had too little time to interact with needy students on a one-to-one basis, and that in some cases they did not get sufficient help from administrators or regular teachers to provide beneficial learning environments and academic resources for their students. The teachers frequently indicated that they felt regular educators and administrators were not always supportive of PL 94–142, a condition that might prevent LD students from getting the full benefit of a wide range of selected services.

A second theme emerging from the data was that working with LD students and designing learning environments that contribute to their growth were the most satisfying and fulfilling aspects of the job. Many of the open-ended comments made by the respondents clearly spoke to the joy of having a unique opportunity to work with a small group of students in a well-defined, structured learning environment. These teachers were able to clearly document learner progress, demonstrating that their professional efforts were paying dividends. The data also seem to indicate that teachers of LD students have ambivalent feelings about their regular education colleagues. Whereas relationships with regular educators, administrators, and support staff were moderate stressors in the rank-ordering process, 20 (25 percent) of the LD respondents cited interaction with special education colleagues as an aspect of job satisfaction. Additionally, when asked for items they would change in their work environment, the teachers of LD students cited improved attitudes by regular educators and school administrators toward the intent of PL 94–142. In short, it is very clear that teachers of LD students very much enjoy working with other special educators in contrast to regular educators, because these colleagues often provide a support base in an otherwise isolated setting.

In a global sense, it appears from these data that the teachers of LD students who responded to this survey were satisfied with their jobs, in particular, working with students who exhibit special learning challenges. What appears to be a critical concern was the necessity of having to work in a physical setting that often confines and restricts the realization of learning goals. Another problem indicated by teachers of LD students was not having sufficient time during the school day to work on IEPs, plan curricular units, or interact with students on a one-to-one basis. There was also a definite concern about the lack of harmonious teaming with other members of the school community including regular educators, administrators, support staff, and parents. The teachers responding to this survey articulated that without a more comprehensive interdisciplinary orientation to educational programming, LD students were not receiving a congruent, synchronized educational program.

Other Studies

In an early study D'Alonzo and Wiseman reported that most resource teachers saw cooperation, planning, and interactions with regular educators as a major problem area (54). In another study, Morsink, Blackhurst, and Williams found that the most significant problems for teachers of LD students were (a) lack of instructional materials; (b) getting regular teachers to understand needs of exceptional children; (c) developing sequential, individual programs for each student; (d) lack of time for planning; and (e) misplacement of children in special classes (55). In another study of resource room teachers, Bensky, Shaw, Gouse, Bates, Dixon, and Beane identified evaluation by supervisors and unclear expectations as contributors to job stress (56).

In 1982, Olson and Matuskey studied 173 teachers of students with specific learning disabilities to determine the strongest job stressors and arrived at items similar to those previously reported (57). These researchers cited excessive paperwork, inadequate salaries, student discipline problems, insufficient planning time, student apathy, and pupil-teacher ratios as the six strongest stressors. In another study, Fimian, Pierson, and McHardy used the Teacher Stress Inventory (TSI) to examine the strongest and most frequently occurring stressful events reported by teachers of LD students (58). Items relating to personal/professional concerns (caseload size, shortchanged personal priorities); and professional dissatisfaction (lacking recognition, needing enhanced status, and inadequate salaries) were identified by respondents as high contributors to stress. Other areas such as classroom management and motivational issues were ranked in the medium range of concerns.

Several consistent concerns become apparent when reviewing the results of investigations addressing teachers of this population. Lack of planning time was identified as a major job stressor; lack of instructional materials, IEPs, relationships with regular educators, and apathetic students were perceived as obstacles to job satisfaction.

Conclusion

Because LD students generally appear to have no overt disability, regular educators can see no tangible indication of a learning disability and become impatient and intolerant of the problems these students experience. Thus, the teacher of LD students faces a major challenge with respect to sensitizing regular educators to the trials and tribulations that these students experience. It is much more difficult to conceptualize something that cannot be seen or touched. Such is the case with this population.

Individuals choose to work with students with learning disabilities knowing in advance that there will be many challenges concerning designing educational programs for students with deficits in knowledge bases and deficiencies in processing information. As is the case with all teachers, apathetic students present barriers to professional success. This might be especially frustrating to teachers of LD students who work with smaller numbers of students and are responsible for closely monitoring their academic progress. A great deal of the satisfaction that accrues from working with exceptional students is the growth that these students undergo as they interact with an individualized learning environment. It would appear that teachers of LD students are not complaining about the time involved in writing individualized programs; they are, however, asserting that there is often insufficient time during the workday to prepare and evaluate these programs.

STRESSORS PECULIAR TO TEACHERS OF BEHAVIORALLY DISORDERED STUDENTS

Scenario

Jodie works in a self-contained classroom with 10 students who have serious emotional, psychological, and social problems. Many of her students have the capacity to do acceptable work in school but their behavioral excesses prevent them from achieving a high measure of academic success. These students are hypersensitive to criticism and often explode verbally and physically when confronted with a frustrating situation. The biggest stress for Jodie is their unpredictability on a daily basis. She is often confused about what her professional role should be. Many of her students desperately need a therapist to sort out their chaotic lives; others need a surrogate parent, someone who exhibits caring and concern in an otherwise troublesome social environment; still others need a high degree of structure in their lives, an individual who consistently enforces rules and expectations; lastly, all the BD students need a good teacher who can help them acquire socially appropriate behaviors as well as academic competencies.

Given the multiple disorders exhibited by these students and the many learning deficits they possess, Jodie often feels tired under the weight of all these responsibilities. Additionally, she is somewhat concerned for her personal safety, fearful that some event may trigger an explosive outburst on the part of one of her students. Often she feels that she is a target for displaced aggression exhibited by several of the more hostile students. Clearly, Jodie has few moments when she can relax. From another perspective she sees herself as a captive in her own classroom. With good reason, she is reluctant to leave her students alone. While she likes her students and feels challenged by the severity of their deficiencies, she is completely exhausted both physically and mentally. Unfortunately, she feels that no other staff member really appreciates what she does or is interested in helping her design programs for her students. Worse yet, most teachers do not like her students, are fearful of their sudden outbursts, and indirectly seem to avoid Jodie just as they do the BD students with whom she works. In this context, Jodie, indeed, feels like a pariah.

The Data Base

Rank Order of Job-Related Stressors

An examination of Table 4.3 indicates that teachers of BD students were most concerned about student needs that were not being met. A second concern was students who present serious behavioral problems, problems that often result in refusal to engage in academic tasks. Lack of assistance from school administrators was a third pressing source of concern. Teachers were least concerned about staff meetings, teacher-pupil ratios, and isolation from colleagues. Paperwork, lack of support from specialized services, lack of time, regular class teacher attitudes, and insufficient resources were ranked in the middle group of stressors.

Table 4.3
Rank Order of Stressors:
Teachers of BD Students
N = 70

1. Students' unmet needs
2. Uncooperative students
3. Unhelpful administrators
4. Nonsupportive parents
5. Paperwork (IEPs)
6. Lack of support from specialized services
7. Lack of preparation time
8. Regular educators' attitudes
9. Insufficient resources
10. Lengthy meetings
11. Large teacher-pupil ratio
12. Isolation from colleagues

Desirable and Undesirable Aspects of the Profession

The research sample of teachers of BD students identified student progress, working with students, and the challenge of arranging learning environments to best meet the needs of their student population as the most enjoyable aspects of their job (Table 4.4). Also mentioned were the relative autonomy to create learning environments and interaction with specific colleagues.

With regard to changes in the workplace, teachers of BD students issued a strong appeal for more help from administrators, more parent involvement, and less paperwork. These teachers also wanted more time for lesson preparation and more cooperation from regular class teachers.

Discussion of Survey Results

As might be expected, of the three groups, teachers of BD students were most concerned about students whose disruptive and uncooperative behavior upset the orderly flow of classroom instruction. Additionally, teachers of BD students did not feel they received sufficient support from building administrators. Undoubtedly, it can be assumed that this criticism may have been targeted toward administrators who failed to back up teachers of BD students in cases of inappropriate, disruptive behavior. This is quite understandable given the volatile nature of these students. Additionally, the fact that teachers of BD students work with students who are often perceived by other school staff as "troublemakers" might lead them more than their colleagues who teach LD or MD students to feel that administrators and supervisors are not sufficiently helpful in providing backup support.

Teachers of BD students also expressed concern about the lack of parental support. Such support is essential in the follow-through programs if there is to be any consistency in the child's environment. When parents do not follow through with suggestions made by teachers of these students, they can seriously compromise any effectiveness the teachers might have in the classroom.

Other Studies

In the Johnson, Gold, and Vickers study, teachers of BD students perceived insufficient and inappropriate supervisory service; insufficient psychological services; fear of physical attacks, verbal threats, and other potential violence by students as more stressful than did teachers of MD and LD students (59). In short, teachers of BD students felt their teaching responsibilities were significantly more stressful than the responsibilities of the other two groups, particularly because of the ever-present

Table 4.4
Desirable and Undesirable Aspects of the Work
Environment: Teachers of BD Students
N = 70

List three aspects of your job that you like

Rank	Item	Frequency	Percent
1	Student progress	39	56%
2	Interaction with students	31	44%
3	Curricular challenge	26	37%
4	Freedom to implement	18	25%
5	Other colleagues	13	18%

If you could change aspects of the environment in which you work, what would these changes be?

Rank	Item	Frequency	Percent
1	More administrative support	32	46%
2	More parent involvement	21	30%
3	Less paperwork	17	24%
4	Increase in planning time	11	16%
5	More cooperation from regular teachers	9	12%

possibility of student-initiated aggression.

As Zabel, Boomer and King pointed out, because of professional role demands, teachers of BD students are frequently isolated from colleagues, and consequently are limited in their opportunities for social and professional support (60). In particular, teachers in itinerant settings may not have an identity with a particular school culture, while teachers in a self-contained setting may not be able to leave their students for collegial interaction.

Conclusion

Teachers of behaviorally disordered students work with a volatile student population. Words such as unpredictable, confrontational, and displaced aggression characterize the students they teach. Clearly, BD students present a wide range of behavioral excesses and deficits, conditions that can arouse negative feelings in their teachers as well as in regular class teachers. In addition to the ever-present challenge in the area of academics, there is the complication of behavioral deviance. Each student represents a potential crisis ready to happen. There is also the need for confirmation that one is doing a satisfactory job—in this instance, that the work of the teacher is paying dividends in the improved academic and social behavior of the BD student. When conditions in the home hamper these efforts, when school officials are reluctant to intervene in cases involving serious inappropriate behaviors, when other teachers avoid contact with BD students as well as their teacher, the potential for job stress is very real. Teachers of BD students rarely get to see the long-term benefits of their ministrations. The input from other sources, in many cases negative and self-destructive, chips away at their efforts. Yet there is always the professional hope that through good instruction, firm limits, and genuine understanding, these students will become less impulsive and more socially responsible.

STRESSORS PECULIAR TO TEACHERS OF MENTALLY DEFICIENT STUDENTS

Scenario

Bill works in a self-contained classroom with 12 MD students in a regular school building. It is a small classroom in the basement of the building, a room that is conspicuously isolated from regular school traffic. At times, Bill is defensive about "his kids." Yes, some of them look different, but he resents the fact that other students and teachers ste-

43

reotype his MD students as "retards." He realizes that some of his students do not have appropriate social skills, but he firmly believes that they need to interact with other members of the school community. He wishes it were not so difficult to have his students integrated into music, art, and physical education classes.

Another thing that bothers Bill is the apathy of some community members with respect to work study programs. Although his students manifest deficiencies in adaptive behavior and may be slower in catching on than other students, Bill feels strongly that if they are to contribute to society and demonstrate independent living skills, they must have opportunities to gain marketable work skills.

Bill feels surrounded by people who disenfranchise his MD students. He wishes other staff members, students, administrators, and community members would have more compassion for these special-needs students. He hopes that someday they will not be called names and will not have to feel they are on the fringe of society.

The Data Base

Rank Order of Job-Related Stressors

An examination of the data (Table 4.5) indicates that the primary concern of teachers of MD students was the individualized educational plans (IEPs) they are required to write for each student by Public Law 94–142. Specifically, involving parents in the IEP process, updating goals based on learner progress, and targeting particular goals unique to the learner rather than generic lifelong goals were addressed as major challenges in developing functional IEPs. Uncooperative students and students' unmet needs were identified as second- and third-rated stressors by participants. Several respondents wrote lengthy narrative comments about the dysfunctional families with whom they were trying to work. Concerns in this area included failure of parents to participate in conferences, to return phone calls, or to respond to written requests. Areas of lesser concern included isolation from colleagues, lengthy meetings, and insufficient resources. Relationships with support staff, regular educators, and teacher-student ratio were ranked in the middle group of stressors.

Desirable and Undesirable Aspects of the Profession

As indicated in Table 4.6, respondents strongly identified working with students and observing their academic progress as the most enjoyable aspects of their job. These teachers also felt that interaction with colleagues provided a stimulating work environment that contributed to professional growth. Additionally, respondents felt the freedom to design innovative instructional materials to best meet the needs of individ-

44

Table 4.5
Rank Order of Stressors:
Teachers of MD Students
N = 82

1. Paperwork (IEPs)
2. Uncooperative students
3. Students' unmet needs
4. Lack of preparation time
5. Nonsupportive parents
6. Unhelpful administrators
7. Large teacher/pupil ratio
8. Lack of support from specialized services
9. Regular educators' attitudes
10. Lengthy meetings
11. Insufficient resources
12. Isolation from colleagues

ual students was a most rewarding aspect of their chosen profession.

As for suggested changes in the workplace, teachers of MD students emphasized the need for better room accommodations, more administrative support, more cooperation from regular teachers, and more planning time to design individual programs. Twenty-three of the respondents articulated a genuine concern about building administrators who tended to thwart rather than support their programs. In addition to assigning teachers of MD students to work in the least desirable physical environment, many respondents felt that building administrators clearly lacked information concerning the best practices and materials for special-needs students. One teacher used the term "isolated island" to describe the lack of support she received regarding the design and implementation of educational programs for her students.

Discussion of Survey Results

First and foremost, teachers of MD students targeted the need for better communication with administrators and regular educators regarding the placement of their students into less restrictive environments as a top priority item. If MD students (mild, moderate, or severe) are to be successfully mainstreamed/integrated into regular education classrooms/environments, more effective ways for bridging communication across the

Table 4.6
Desirable and Undesirable Aspects of the Work
Environment: Teachers of MD Students
N = 82

	List three aspects of your job that you like				If you could change aspects of the environment in which you work, what would these changes be?		
Rank	Item	Frequency	Percent	Rank	Item	Frequency	Percent
1	Interaction with students	62	76%	1	Improve physical environment	27	33%
2	Evidence of student progress	38	46%	2	More administrative support	23	28%
3	Interaction with colleagues	31	38%	3	More cooperation from regular teachers	11	13%
4	Freedom to implement	20	24%	4	More planning time	9	9%

disciplines and professional staff must be found. Roles and responsibilities of each educator must be more clearly defined, and procedures and time lines for implementing transitions must be better articulated. Well-entrenched attitudes that handicapped MD students are the sole responsibility of special educators (the "yours" vs. "ours" phenomenon) must undergo significant change. The lack of administrative support in a variety of areas including the mainstreaming/integration process was articulated by over 38 percent of MD teachers responding in this survey. As one teacher succinctly put it, "I wish we had an administrator who puts as high a priority on specialized programs as he does on talented and gifted programs."

The teachers of MD students also identified writing IEPs as a very stressful aspect of their job. This factor, coupled with other priority concerns such as students' unmet needs and lack of preparation time, seems to reflect a sincere desire to design educational programs that would maximally benefit the MD student population. Additionally, the data indicate that, regardless of the complexity of the sensory, motor, behavioral, or medical situation of students, teachers of MD students clearly perceived these differences as a major professional challenge and expressed a strong commitment to design educational programs that accommodate the unique learning needs of each student. As one teacher observed, "It is a pleasure to get up in the morning and look forward to what I consider a pleasant, rewarding profession, knowing that I make a considerable difference in the future of each of these youngsters' lives."

Other Studies

In an early study examining areas of satisfaction and dissatisfaction in teaching among teachers of mentally retarded students as contrasted with regular educators, Jones found that the kinds of concerns expressed by special and regular elementary teachers were not significantly different (61). At the secondary level, however, regular teachers saw themselves as having greater rapport with their colleagues than teachers of MD students. The greatest difference between the two groups appeared in the area of curricular issues. When special educators are in a regular school, Jones suggests that they often see themselves as having lower status within the school hierarchy and that regular teachers have little understanding of or appreciation for what they do. Professional morale is greatly improved when other special educators are present and the building principal is sensitive to the unique problems of the teachers of mentally deficient students.

Conclusion

Teachers of MD students do not want regular educators and specialized support staff to operate on the assumption that only the former are responsible for designing and providing an educational environment for their students. Respondents to the authors' survey were rather adamant in stressing the necessity for more administrative support, particularly in the successful fulfillment of the mainstreaming component of PL 94–142. Teachers of MD students do not want their classrooms to become "isolated islands," nor do they want their students to become disenfranchised from the overall educational environment. These teachers stressed the need for bridging the gap between regular and special education, thereby providing more opportunities for their students to be integrated with "regular" students in as many curricular/extracurricular areas as possible.

Lastly, teachers of MD students were somewhat distressed by the overwhelming volume of paperwork involved in providing appropriate learning environments for their students. They also expressed concern about lack of parental support. It was very clear, however, from the authors' survey, that these teachers very much enjoyed the challenges of working with MD students and derived job satisfaction from seeing their students make academic and social progress.

JOB STRESS AND TEACHERS OF THE PHYSICALLY HANDICAPPED

Although this monograph focuses mainly on job stressors experienced by teachers of MD, LD, and BD students, the authors believe that many of the problems discussed in Chapter 4 are also relevant to educators who work with students who are physically handicapped. Among the common stress provokers for all special educators would be IEPs, emissions of inappropriate student behavior, slow rates of social and academic progress, and frustrating relationships with regular educators and colleagues. Unlike children with mild handicaps who evidence no visible indicators of special needs, however, the physical disability handicap is readily apparent to other children and educators.

Special educators who work with severely and profoundly handicapped, cerebral-palsied, and other children experiencing physical disabilities may have additional stressors that might be somewhat unique—for example, locomotion and speech. Many physically handicapped students may be confined to wheelchairs, while others may have difficulty in walking. Frequently educators are required to assist them by engaging in large amounts of lifting, pulling, or pushing. Clearly, all routines and transitions become much more complicated. Simply going out to recess with eight nonambulatory students can be a major challenge. In these instances, it is crucial that educational and recreational facilities be adapted to meet the physical needs of these students. Elevators, ramps, and abundant support staff can do much to abate stress. In addition, communication can present some special challenges if students are nonverbal.

Lastly, we would imagine that professionals working with severely physically and multiply handicapped students may at times have to be extremely patient with regard to student progress. While special educators in general may be frustrated by the slow gains manifested by their students, this situation may be intensified for those working with students who present multiple handicaps.

Whereas much of the discussion in this monograph has a distinct relationship to the special educator working with physically handicapped students, there might be much merit in additional writings and research that focus specifically on professionals who work with these students on a daily basis in a number of settings, some integrated and some not.

JOB STRESS AND RURAL SPECIAL EDUCATORS

The problems discussed thus far become even more hazardous for professional health when we consider the unique challenges faced by rural educators. Three factors tend to place rural special educators at risk with regard to job stress.

First, there is the numbing reality that results from geographic and psychological isolation. In addition to working with all categories of special needs students, the rural special educator is often required to make frequent visits to various school buildings, buildings that are often at opposite ends of the district. Furthermore, working in an isolated setting means that an important link to role clarification and job satisfaction— collegial networks with other staff members—is often lacking. This would be an especially acute situation for first-year special educators who desperately need socializing experiences and the sharing of pedagogical insights.

Second, rural special educators may work with large numbers of students of varying ages. This factor, coupled with the mix of LD, BD, and MD students in one classroom environment, may present serious problems with respect to classroom management and the successful delivery of individual education programs. Unfortunately, the contemporary situation portrayed here bears little resemblance to the one-room schoolhouse with its images of peer tutoring and cooperative support systems.

A third factor contributing to the stress of rural special educators is the overall lack of accessibility to resources that are critical to successful job performance. These resources include support personnel, the availability of curricular materials, and the presence of adaptive technology and equipment. The major impediment to accessibility, of course, is geographic isolation. For example, in order to obtain necessary materials, rural special educators may have to travel considerable distances to gain input about contemporary technology and innovative curricular materials. The distance factor also makes it difficult for support personnel to visit their classrooms. It is not difficult to envision a scenario where it would be distinctly advantageous for the rural special educator to be an assertive individual who champions mainstreaming, lobbies hard for the integration of special-needs students into least restrictive environments, and makes frequent demands for supplies and equipment. All this is often done without the help of a support team or ancillary personnel.

5. ORGANIZATIONAL/PERSONAL STRATEGIES FOR COPING WITH STRESS

INTRODUCTION

The teachers who remain special educators for a considerable number of years have probably become very adept at managing job-related stress. It is reasonable to surmise that these experienced teachers have found suitable outlets and activities to defuse the frustrations of the everyday world of work.

As part of our study focusing on special educators and job stress, the authors investigated ways these teachers coped with job stress. We selected a Q-sort format with 16 cells (62) to aid in identifying stress-coping mechanisms. We requested participants to rank the 16 strategies for dealing with stress, ranging from items perceived as "most like me" to those perceived as "least like me."

This chapter discusses organizational strategies for developing effective coalitions among school staff, as well as individual initiatives, to reduce job-related stress. Chapter 6 presents a detailed analysis of 10 strategies that individuals can use to cope with stress.

THE DATA BASE

Since there were many similarities in the ways in which teachers of LD, BD, and MD students responded to the Q-sort instrument, the results are reviewed as a composite of all three student populations.

In terms of the overall research sample (see Table 5.1), the respondents identified the use of humor as the most prominent strategy for dealing with job-related stress; they also identified focusing on one's accomplishments—emphasis on positives—as a preferred strategy. A third coping strategy by special educators in general was active participation in a variety of hobbies, specifically activities that are unrelated to the everyday responsibilities of the teaching profession. Additional activities such as lesson planning, exercise, and reading were seen as "like me" ways of handling job stress.

The strategies least frequently used by special educators to alleviate stress in the workplace were late arrival at work, thoughts about leaving the profession, confrontation with other staff members, and joining a support group. Other coping mechanisms seldom identified by respondents to combat stress included complaining to administrators and supervisors, yelling at students, and overeating/overdrinking.

Table 5.1
Ways of Dealing with Job-Related Stress by
Teachers of LD, BD, and MD Students

Special Education Population	Most Like Me	Very Much Like Me	Like Me	Undecided	Unlike Me	Very Much Unlike Me	Most Unlike Me
BD Teachers	Laugh/humor	Hobbies Focus on accomplishments	Read Plan Solicit positive comments	Overeat Ventilate frustration Exercise Leave profession	Complain to administration Support group Use punitive measures	Yell at students Arrive late	Confront other staff members
LD Teachers	Focus on accomplishments	Hobbies Laugh/humor	Exercise Read Yell at students	Support group Plan Solicit positive comments Use punitive controls	Complain to administration Ventilate frustration Leave profession	Confront other staff members Overeat	Arrive late
MD Teachers	Laugh/humor	Read Focus on accomplishments	Plan Hobbies Exercise	Yell at students Overeat Ventilate frustration Solicit positive comments	Confront other staff members Support group Use punitive measures	Arrive late Complain to administration	Leave profession

DISCUSSION OF SURVEY RESULTS

A major theme emerging from these data is that special educators employ a variety of positive techniques for dealing with job stress such as humor, focusing on professional success experiences, and enjoying hobbies. Special educators, however, appear to be reluctant to confront other staff members and building/district administrators about aspects of their work that they find distressing or problematic. And, unlike the results of some other studies (63), it was refreshing to note that a majority of these teachers indicated that leaving the profession was a "not-like-me" choice in the Q-sort format.

The fact that special educators in this sample did not see themselves as active confronters with respect to problem areas related to job stress is an interesting finding. According to the data presented in Chapter 4, a primary concern reported by teachers of LD, BD, and MD students was the lack of professional dialogue and support from other members of the professional community with whom they work in close proximity: regular teachers, specialized support staff, and administrators. This lack of collaboration can seriously jeopardize the spirit of mainstreaming and can have serious effects on students with special learning problems. Ways of enhancing team cohesiveness and techniques for bridging communication across disciplines need to be identified so that a more effective interdisciplinary orientation toward exceptionalities may be taken.

It was also interesting to note that special educators in the Dedrick/Raschke research sample did not identify support groups as a way of coping with job stress. One would suspect that this particular group of teachers has become accustomed to professional isolation from one another and may resort to individual self-help strategies before engaging in group-type structures. It does seem reasonable, however, that if a teaming effort is critical to providing appropriate services for exceptional children, then special and regular educators need to bridge differences and seek out common missions. The notion of a building support group would have special relevance for first-year special educators who clearly need a mentor and for well-seasoned veterans who might benefit from the vim and vigor exhibited by the junior faculty.

OTHER STUDIES

When Johnson, Gold, and Vickers asked special educators to list activities they found beneficial in guarding against stress, six items they rated relatively high were: (1) exercise programs, (2) outdoor recreation, (3) confiding in a significant other, (4) setting realistic goals, (5) self-support, and (6) peer support (64). These items were not ranked in any particular order. Most of them are self-initiatives but at least two emphasize the importance of the role that other people—significant others and colleagues—play in maintaining a healthy posture to withstand the challenges presented by working with exceptional children. Three other suggestions mentioned by these researchers were time management, communication skills, and the ability to resolve potentially explosive situations. The last item would undoubtedly focus on conflict resolution strategies.

Dunham emphasized that staff "working groups"—meeting on a regular basis to consider agenda items of mutual concern—were a good vehicle for increasing skills of interprofessional communication and cooperation (65). Since special educators in the authors' survey frequently mentioned specialized services and regular educators as major sources of stress, it seems logical to conclude that if mainstreaming is to be successful, professionals who represent different areas of expertise must work together to provide optimal learning environments for all children, including those who have exceptional needs.

Schwab, Jackson, and Shuler presented some comprehensive strategies to reduce burnout caused by factors such as role conflict and ambiguity, a sense of powerlessness, low collegiality, and minimal participation in decision making (66). These included

1. Establishing clear lines of authority and responsibility
2. Soliciting teacher input for decision making
3. Facilitating social support groups
4. Involving staff in the selection process
5. Involving teachers in the evaluation process by providing opportunities for goal setting and self-evaluation
6. Encouraging mentoring relationships between veteran faculty and beginning teachers.

All six strategies emphasize the importance of a collegial working environment in which special educators feel they are instrumental in making decisions that directly affect them. To help bridge the alleged gap between regular and special educators, it would seem essential that each teacher have a clear understanding of the nature of his/her roles and functions. With regard to a smoothly functioning school environment, the building administrator is definitely the key. This individual can allow for participatory decision making by enhancing the ownership teachers have in maintaining a productive, professionally satisfying school environment. The idea of teachers having a voice in selecting new teachers as well as in establishing a bond between experienced and beginning teachers makes good sense because these activities directly contribute to staff morale.

Although it is often difficult to implement organizational change concerning working hours, planning periods, teacher assistants, and student-teacher ratio, Weiskopf offers nine practical suggestions for reducing the amount of stress teachers experience on a personal level (67):

1. Know in advance what the job requires in terms of emotional demands.
2. Set realistic goals for yourself and your students.
3. Delegate routine work to volunteers or aides.
4. Avoid becoming isolated from other staff members.
5. Break up the direct contact with students through team teaching, learning centers, etc.
6. Remain intellectually active off the job.
7. Engage in physical exercise.
8. Interject newness and variety to offset routine while on the job.
9. Participate in hobbies and activities not directly related to the job.

Some of these suggestions are also dealt with more thoroughly in Chapter 6.

Investigating why some teachers burn out and others do not, Holt, Fine, and Tollefson found that teachers experiencing high stress and high burnout tended to cope with stress by using passive strategies, such as venting frustration on others (68). Additionally, teachers in this group tended to be in poor physical health, alienated themselves from others, and demonstrated an external locus of control. Teachers in the high stress, low burnout group used more active coping strategies such as humor and involvement in a hobby. They were generally healthier as a group and had a more internal locus of control. These researchers highlighted three overall factors that seem to contribute to stress hardiness: (1) commitment and involvement in many aspects of one's life, (2) the acceptance of change as a reality of life, and (3) the belief that one can control the course of events in one's life. These three factors seem to be integral aspects of personality that may be significantly shaped by events experienced in the formative years of life. Indeed, many of these characteristics could be representative of the individual's philosophy toward life in general. If the areas of commitment, challenge, and control are crucial for developing the toughness to ride through high-stress days, then perhaps more courses at the pre-professional level and more workshops at the professional level should be designed to help special educators develop an orientation toward life that emphasizes an internal locus of openness to new experiences, and full involvement in private and professional activities.

Focusing on organizational strategies that could be used to prevent or reduce the incidence of burnout, Gold offered several suggestions, some of which rely heavily on the abilities and sensitivities of administrative staff:

1. Implementing a level of challenge and stimulation for creativity on a continuous level.

2. Providing direction, attainable goals, and programs which enable fulfillment for individuals and the institution.

3. Encouraging mentors for junior faculty members during the first years of their academic career.

4. Rewarding those who have made a significant contribution.

5. Providing assistance where needed to encourage faculty toward greater creativity and productivity.

6. Encouraging administrators to support and challenge faculty endeavors.

7. Providing faculty with increased levels of respect, security, authority. (69, p. 144)

Many of these suggestions have a direct relationship to previous discussions concerning job satisfaction. The variables that increase our sense of competence and achievement contribute to our professional self-worth. In addition, it is important for teachers to be acknowledged within the organizational structure for a job well done.

CONCLUSION

The data from the authors' research with teachers of LD, BD, and MD students, coupled with the findings of the studies discussed in this chapter, provide some valuable insights into ways to offset job stress. Three themes seem to appear throughout the literature base.

First, there is a clear indication that to offset job stress and enhance professional satisfaction it is important that special educators have a keen sense of job autonomy. This does not mean that they work in isolation from other educators—on the contrary. It does mean, however, that within the confines of the resource room, etc., the teacher is in charge. It also means that teachers have reasonable authority in the design of curricular materials since this is a fundamental area of their instructional expertise.

The second theme is organizational involvement. This means that special educators need to be given opportunities to voice their opinions, at times expressing professional grievances. Such opportunities should occur in a climate free from retaliation and petty bureaucracy. Several of the studies on teacher burnout allude to the special educator's sense of isolation within the school hierarchy. These educators need to see themselves as integral components of the school environment with channels open to express professional concerns.

The third theme is the instrumental role that colleagues play in maintaining a work environment that ideally emphasizes collegiality and sharing of resources. Since staffings and teamings are realities for special educators, providing them with experiences that increase possibilities for open communication and decrease barriers to cooperation seems important. It is also important that colleagues get together every now and then to reinforce each other for a job well done.

6. PREVENTIVE AND REMEDIAL STRATEGIES FOR COPING WITH STRESS

INTRODUCTION

"Beware! Teaching special education may be hazardous to your health." Perhaps this statement should be typed in bold red ink on all special education teaching certifications. The unique demands of the special educational professional lay the groundwork for stress and burnout to take its toll. Unquestionably, those who work with special-needs students face extra responsibilities and pressures. Let's look at the following questions:

- Do you often feel overworked and underpaid?
- Do you have 10 or more hours of paperwork overdue and in need of completion?
- Do you have five or more meetings with parents, teachers, or administrators scheduled before or after school during the next week?
- Do you feel alienated from the school in which you teach, from your regular education colleagues, or from the administration?
- Are you overly exhausted, irritable, or depressed at the end of the school day?

If your answer to one or more of these questions is yes, you are a teacher under stress and you may be a candidate for burnout.

In order to cope with stress effectively, it is extremely important that special educators complete a self-inventory to target specific stress contributors. *KNOWING ONESELF* in terms of what produces tension and what produces relaxation is crucial. Chart 6.1 displays some common sources of stress as well as indexes of ownership. Recognizing these sources can help special educators implement appropriate preventative and remedial strategies. On Chart 1, identify the degree to which each of a variety of variables is contributing to your stress. Rate each of these 10 sources of stress on a scale of 1–3—3 denotes a high degree of stress, 2 a moderate degree of stress, 1 a manageable degree of stress. Once these specific variables are identified, the next step is to determine problem ownership. This entails pinpointing who owns the problem and the degree to which self, other teachers, support staff, administrators, parents, and the community contribute to the situation.

Chart 6.1
Stress

Sources of Burnout for the Special Educator	Self-Rating* Degree of Stress	Ownership (Who Owns the Problem)**					
		Community	Parents	Admin- istrators	Professional Support Staff	Other Teachers	Self
Work over-load							
Little support							
Not appre-ciated							
Unrealistic expectations							
Lack of growth							
Isolation							
Job demands							
Powerless-ness							
Student behavior							
Peer relationships							

*For self-rating, using a scale of 1–3, 3 denotes a high degree of stress, 2 a moderate degree of stress, 1 a manageable degree of stress. Scoring: 10–17 = mildly stressed; 18–25 = moderately stressed; 26–30 = severely stressed.

**For each source of burnout, indicate problem ownership with an X in the appropriate column(s).

NEGATIVE ATTITUDES AND SELF-FULFILLING PROPHECIES

Clearly, special educators do not have control over many of the variables impacting their workday. However, attitude and the unique manner in which each person conceptualizes a problem play a crucial role in problem resolution. The proverbial water glass described as "half full" or "half empty" exemplifies such a phenomenon.

Many teachers go to school each day anticipating "gloom and doom" in their encounters with the students with whom they work. After all, "unpredictability" is probably the single best descriptor of most special education classrooms. For teachers of students with special needs, it is very easy to articulate a pessimistic orientation when routines and activities rarely go as planned day after day. Unfortunately, negative expectations can evolve into self-fulfilling prophecies. When one begins to anticipate and expect that the worst will happen, it often does. Let's look at some of the characteristics of teachers who are caught up in the "catch-em'-being-naughty" cycle. Do you know a special educator who does any of the following:

- Repeatedly criticizes a student's behavior in front of other students?
- Regularly punishes the group for the actions of a few?
- Ignores the good things students do?
- Expects students to do their worst in any given situation?
- Encourages students to tattle on each other?
- Emphasizes competitive activities so that there are always losers?

Research has demonstrated the tremendous value in the special education classroom of catching students behaving appropriately, rather than focusing on inappropriate behaviors. In fact, a 4 to 1 ratio is targeted as an indicator of effective teaching—that is, catching students behaving at four times the rate they are caught misbehaving (70). The "criticism trap" may be described as "flypaper" to avoid; the teacher's attention and time should be awarded to those engaging in appropriate behaviors rather than to those misbehaving. For special education teachers, avoiding the criticism trap is a major challenge. Unfortunately, because of the very nature of the students with whom they work, focusing on inappropriate behaviors often becomes extremely easy. After all, many of these students have been placed in special education classrooms as a result of their high rate of inappropriate behavior. A good rule to follow to avoid the criticism trap is to—

> Let the misbehavior of one student be your cue to reinforce another student exhibiting the alternative desirable response.

All teachers clearly feel better about themselves and their teaching if they can avoid the criticism trap. Making an effort to catch each student engaging in a desirable activity at least once each day is a laudable goal. It is amazing how much better teachers can feel about themselves when they enthusiastically deliver positive encouragement to others.

The remainder of this chapter describes 10 specific strategies that teachers can use to manage the stress in their lives and to avoid burnout.

STRESS MANAGEMENT STRATEGIES

As long as stress-producing conditions exist, it will be necessary for educators to find ways to avoid burnout. Just as there are many causes and sources of stress, so are there many prevention and intervention strategies to combat it. Some are constructive approaches that emphasize a healthy orientation—for example, maintaining diet and exercise. Others are destructive—for example, overeating or venting frustrations on students.

To overcome the ill effects of distress, the most important thing teachers can do is to take charge of their own lives. Following are 10 proactive and constructive approaches teachers can use to reduce stress and preserve their teaching effectiveness—diet and exercise, relaxation techniques, social support systems, goal setting, creative problem solving, time management, networking, self-talk, stroking, and GTMs.

Diet and Exercise

Not only does a nourishing diet keep the body fit to resist stress better, but current research indicates that there are direct links between what people eat and the way they feel emotionally (71). The following dietary and exercise guidelines are recommended for stress reduction:

- Avoid foods with artificial additives, flavorings, and colorings (72).
- Avoid excessive use of liquor and caffeine. Caffeine used in excess produces symptoms that are indistinguishable from anxiety neurosis because of its harmful effect on the central nervous system (73).
- Avoid faddish diets and quick weight-loss programs. These programs can be hazardous to your health (74). Long-term weight loss is maintained by regular exercise and good eating habits.
- Avoid smoking altogether if you possibly can. It is dangerous to your health (75).
- Change some of your eating habits to reduce your intake of saturated fat, processed sugar, cholesterol, and salt. These foods have

been linked to various diseases including cancer, heart disease, diabetes, and hypertension (76).

- Get some form of daily exercise. Walking, jogging, or some other kind of active exercise will help dissipate the tension after a tough day in the classroom (77).

Diet and physical fitness are two important aspects of the teacher's daily life. Look at the Diet and Physical Fitness Questionnaires that follow and rate yourself. Answer each item yes or no. Then use the rating scale to determine what kind of shape you are in. The more yes responses you provided, the better equipped your body is to cope with stress.

Relaxation Techniques

Many standard stress-reduction techniques such as yoga, meditation, and self-hypnosis are very effective (78). Biofeedback techniques have also been helpful in reducing individual symptoms (79). There are some relatively inexpensive tools on the commercial market today that are designed to give feedback about an individual's relative stress levels. Examples include stress dots (Mindbody, Inc., 50 Maple Place, Manhasset, NY 11030 [516-365-7722], and stress meters (Conscious Living Foundation, P.O. Box 9, Drain, OR 97435 [503-836-2358]). Additional resources such as *Structured Exercises in Stress Management*, Volumes 1, 2, and 3 (80, 81, 82), provide teachers with a vast array of relaxation techniques.

Other techniques for reducing tension and stress are described in the literature. One specific technique, "thought halting," can be effective when teachers find themselves besieged by counterproductive or negative thoughts. This technique requires the individual to simply listen to an inner voice that yells "stop" or to couple the command with a visual image of a stop sign. Such a momentary pause enables the individual to regroup and rechannel thoughts along a more constructive avenue (83).

Another technique, "thematic imagery," has also been found effective in stress reduction (84). Using this technique, individuals take themselves on guided journeys filled with visions of relaxed environments. The following is an example:

Position your body so you are sitting comfortably in your chair. Let your eyelids fall slowly until they are closed. Take several deep breaths of air. Let go of any tightness in your forehead. Let your jaw relax. Notice whether there is any tension in your shoulders, and let it go. Continue relaxing your body and enjoying that warm comfortable feeling. You are on a quiet, sunny beach. The ocean waves softly splash against the shore. You can smell the breeze. The sand feels warm and good. A fresh breeze of air bounces across your face. All feelings of

Diet Questionnaire

Answer each question yes or no.

1. Do you generally feel energetic? _____
2. Can you run up a short flight of stairs without becoming out of breath? _____
3. Do you exercise for 20 minutes, three times a week? _____
4. After running in place for three minutes, is your pulse rate less than 120 beats per minute? _____
5. Can you hold your breath for 45 seconds? _____
6. Can you do 20 sit-ups? _____
7. Can you walk a mile at a fast pace without becoming exhausted? _____
8. When you pinch your waistline, is the skin fold an inch or less? _____

TOTAL _____

Physical Fitness Questionnaire

Answer each question yes or no.

1. Does your weight fall in the normal range? _____
2. Do you eat balanced meals? _____
3. Do you avoid excessive use of alcohol, coffee, or tobacco? _____
4. Do you eat some breakfast every day? _____
5. Do you drink six to eight glasses of water a day? _____
6. Do you eat healthy snack foods daily? _____
7. Does your diet contain roughage each day? _____
8. Do you avoid excessive use of sweets? _____

TOTAL _____

Give yourself 1 point for each yes response. Compare your total score in each area with the following rating scale:

8–7 = A great shape!
6–5 = Very good
4–3 = Satisfactory
2–1 = Poor
0 = Need immediate attention

tightness and muscle constrictions in your body are beginning to vanish. (85)

Imagery exercises have been demonstrated to alter physiological responses as well as to modify emotions (86).

Progressive relaxation is a technique that helps promote deep relaxation. It can be extremely beneficial if done before school begins, at lunch, or after arriving home. The exercise described below takes five to ten minutes.

1. Take 10 slow, deep breaths. Each time you breathe out imagine that you are relaxing.

2. Think first of your scalp. Wiggle it; now relax it. Feel the tingly sensation it produces on your head.

3. Now think of your face muscles and relax them. Let all the tension go.

4. Raise your shoulders slightly. Lower them slowly and exhale at the same time. As they lower, feel yourself relaxing more completely. Your neck, shoulders, and chest are relaxed.

5. This relaxed feeling spreads down your arms to your fingers. Your fingers are without tension. They are heavy.

6. With each breath you become more and more relaxed. Take five slow deep breaths.

7. Now relax your abdominal section. These muscles become very relaxed.

8. Breathe in and, as you do, tighten the muscles in your legs. As you exhale, relax your legs. There is a pleasant feeling over your entire body.

9. Raise your toes, but only slightly because you are so relaxed. Now let them go down.

10. Feel the calmness over your entire body. No tension remains. Just enjoy it. Allow yourself a few minutes just to enjoy this relaxed, pleasant state.

Social Support Systems

Everyone needs to have contact with others in some mutually supportive way. The claim "I can handle this myself" often leads to additional isolation, and isolation can intensify stress. Reaching out to others who may be experiencing the same stressors can provide comfort. Good openers when seeking support from colleagues include statements such as, "I was wondering if you could give me some feedback as to why I might be feeling so overwhelmed," or "What kinds of things do you do to relieve this mounting stress and tension?"

Some teachers lack systems that are adequate for sharing the thoughts, feelings, and actions that are part of normal human behavior. Learning to expand and use support systems and develop techniques for reducing feelings of isolation is essential. Some ways of doing this follow.

- Get involved with or form a support group within the district. School counselors and psychologists are excellent sources of support and can help identify alternative support groups.

- Identify others who enjoy similar interests and hobbies that are unrelated to teaching. Join a bridge club or participate in a joggers' group.

- Take a short course in an area of interest that appeals to you. Vow to yourself that you will attempt to cultivate one new friendship with someone in the group.

Some teachers have adequate support systems but fail to use them sufficiently. This can leave them without the interpersonal feedback so essential to personal growth. Such thoughts as "I don't want to bother her" or "He has enough problems" can prevent the use of a support system. One way to minimize the fear of overtaxing others is to focus on lighter, perhaps more humorous, topics. "The silly thing Johnny said" or "the ridiculous look on Mary's face" can provide the impetus for a good chuckle. Laughing with others can be therapeutic.

Goal Setting

Some teachers experience stress as a result of failing to attain goals that, practically speaking, were not attainable from the start. When setting goals, teachers should clearly identify what they want to accomplish and realistically assess their ability to reach those goals. They should not unwittingly plan for failure. The goal-setting checklist that follows contains items known to be useful and effective in helping teachers achieve at their maximum potential.

Goal-Setting Checklist for Teaching Expectations

Answer each question *yes, sometimes,* or *no.*

1. Do you set short-term goals that may be accomplished daily, as well as long-term goals that may take considerably longer periods of time to accomplish? _____

2. Do your short-term goals target small incremental gains depicting realistic learner outcomes? _____

3. Are your goals realistic in targeting accomplishments that can be achieved? _____

4. Do you state your goals in a positive framework targeting what you will do rather than what you will not do? _____

5. Do you set a time frame for evaluating your goals to determine progress being made? _____

6. Do you have a checklist of items to provide a tangible, visible permanent product of what you have accomplished? _____

7. Do you set up a positive reward for yourself when you have made a major accomplishment? _____

8. Do you review accomplishments that have accrued as frequently as you review goals that need to be addressed? _____

9. Do you share your goals and accomplishments with a colleague or peer? _____

10. Do you have a folder containing accomplishments and goals achieved that you can quickly review when you experience an extremely frustrating day? _____

The more "yes" and "sometimes" responses you provided, the more likely you are to focus on positive accomplishments rather than on dismal failures.

Creative Problem Solving

When a problem or dilemma arises, it is extremely important to approach it with an open mind and creatively generate alternatives, each of which might be selected as a solution. Identifying the pros and cons of each alternative can be a valuable exercise in narrowing down the options available and selecting the one that has the highest probability of success. Mentally, and unconsciously, people go through this cognitive exercise daily as they make routine decisions. What to wear, which reading group to take first, etc., are simple dilemmas teachers typically resolve without using a more overt systematic problem-solving orientation. The more solutions that can be generated initially, the greater the menu from which to select a solution. Using the immediate environment and resources to help solve a problem is, of course, the ideal situation. For example, one teacher recently described a most creative way in which she handled some of the excessive paperwork accumulating on her desk.

Overwhelmed with the task of designing a questionnaire surveying faculty and staff on a particular issue, this creative teacher decided to involve her students in the activity. She explained her mission to them and solicited their help. After dividing the students into small groups, she asked each group to develop five questions addressing a specific topic for the survey. Then she compiled the questions from each group and refined the completed questionnaire. When the questionnaires were completed by faculty and staff, the students were involved in tabulating the results and formulating the recommendations. The teacher indicated that not only did she accomplish the dreaded mission that had been administratively assigned to her, but her students gained a great deal from the project. Not only did they learn the rudiments of designing a questionnaire and tabulating the results, but they learned how parts fit together to make up a whole, the value of diversified labor, and how each person's part is important to the outcome of the whole.

This teacher took what appeared to be an overwhelming task, creatively addressed solutions for accomplishing it, and constructively involved her students in activities to achieve the ends. In short, the teacher who felt she was dealt lemons simply made lemonade.

Time Management

Teachers frequently feel overwhelmed by too much to do and too little time in which to do it. Good time management skills can be beneficial in reducing these stresses. As Sisley indicates, "'The goal of time management is to maximize production capabilities and minimize the time you waste'' (87, p. 75). Thus, the mission of the special educator is to get as much necessary and important work done as quickly and with as little stress as possible. Cohen and Hart-Hester have identified the following keys to effective time management (88):

- Make a list of matters needing attention and rank order the items according to their importance and deadlines. As an item is accomplished, check it off.
- Design a work area for yourself in the classroom that is isolated from others. An ideal area faces two blank walls that can easily be partitioned by a divider.

- Develop forms for speeding up and recording notes on conferences, observations, meeting times, and teaching suggestions. Using this format, you need only fill in the preestablished blanks.

- Perform tasks that require similar materials and resources at one sitting. This reduces the amount of time wasted shuffling papers and files. Establishing priorities in a systematic fashion and clearly delineating accomplishments can yield a renewed sense of self-worth and self-control.

- Redirect sidetracked meetings by raising a question that will gain everyone's attention and refocus the discussion. Valuable time is frequently wasted in meetings.

When asked where the time went, many special educators are unable to target how they spent the 480 minutes scheduled for the typical workday. Further, many special educators find that their total week consists entirely of work or work-related activities; little time is set aside for recreational or relaxing activities. A systematic approach to time analysis is one viable solution that can help these teachers see how they are spending their waking hours. The Time Allocation Chart that follows is designed to help teachers target the actual hours spent in various activities each day (Column A). More importantly, teachers need to identify the desired number of hours to be allocated for the various activities (Column B). Clearly, the greater the discrepancy between columns A and B (Column C), the greater the degree of job stress experienced by the special educator related to time-management strategies.

Once the teacher can identify areas of significant discrepancy between actual and desired time allocations, plans for adjusting imbalances can be made and goals established. Additionally, ways to facilitate the adjustment of time allocations need to be brainstormed, options evaluated, and plans for action operationalized.

Networking

Working with the significant others in students' lives can generate a reservoir of resources to tap as needed in emergency situations (89, 90). Such a network consists of individuals who have had previous contact with the student and a general interest in his or her well-being. For example, a juvenile delinquent's support system might consist of a parole officer, a minister, a school counselor, a parent, a relative, a school psychologist, a teacher, and an interested neighbor. Networking consists of pulling together these significant others and collectively forming a plan of action to provide direction and support for a needy young person. It is a valuable tool in stress reduction, for it provides teachers the backup support so desperately needed in crisis situations. With a network in

Time Allocation Analysis

Write the number of hours you actually spend each day on each activity in Column A, and the number of hours you would like to spend each day on each activity in Column B. Then subtract the figure in Column B from the figure in Column A and write the difference in Column C.

A	B	C	D
Actual	Desired	Discrepancy	Activities
			Hours spent in direct instruction daily
			Hours spent in school meetings, conferences, etc.
			Hours spent in planning daily class activities
			Hours spent on paperwork (e.g., IEPs, lesson plans)
			Hours spent on school-related activities at home
			Hours devoted to home responsibilities
			Hours spent with family and friends
			Hours engaged in some physical activity
			Hours spent on yourself (e.g., hobbies, alone time)

place, rather than feeling they are fighting the battle alone, teachers can gain genuine comfort in the thought that '"We're all in this together."

Additionally, special educators need to identify and utilize all available human resources to their maximum potential. The extra time to train a teacher assistant or a secretary to handle some additional responsibilities may indeed be worthwhile. Training students or parent volunteers as classroom aides can result in greatly increased instructional time without increasing the teacher's work load. Students can also help each other with instructional activities. Peer tutoring—students helping each other with schoolwork and sharing strategies for remembering information—can be an extremely useful educational tool. It can help to reduce the strain of "too much to do and too little time to do it in" for the teacher.

Many special educators are unaware of the professional support personnel available to help them assess, program, instruct, and evaluate special-needs students. Consequently, they are not adequately utilizing these staff members and are unaware of help that may be readily available. The following is a list of staff and services available to most special educators:

A. School Psychologist
B. Physical Therapist
C. Occupational Therapist
D. Speech Clinician
E. Consultant

F. Social Worker
G. Strategist
H. Nurse
I. Audiologist

In each of the following nine situations, identify the staff member listed above who would be the best service provider by placing the appropriate letter in the blank.

_____ 1. Susan complains of a stomachache and frequently goes to the bathroom.

_____ 2. Mark is unable to go downstairs rotating a different foot for each subsequent step.

_____ 3. Sally continues to complain about bad dreams and seems unduly afraid in a variety of situations.

_____ 4. Tom is not making any progress whatsoever in reading and you just don't know what to do.

_____ 5. Ricky is having a horrendous time mastering scissors cutting and is not making progress.

_____ 6. Bill cannot differentiate between the words *cut* and *cat* and multiples of similar words.

_____ 7. Sammy always talks in a high squeaky voice and you cannot seem to get him to lower the tone.

_____ 8. Tammy is having difficulty in her mainstreamed class and you have exhausted your repertoire of ways to help her.

_____ 9. Jeff smells of urine every day, and even though you have talked to him and implemented a motivational system, things just are not improving.

Key: 1–H, 2–B, 3–A, 4–E, 5–C, 6–I, 7–D, 8–G, 9–F

Using a support team to help resolve what appear to be unsurmountable obstacles in the classroom can do much to reduce stress and share responsibility equally among all educational staff members. With regard to teaching handicapped learners, remember that the whole may indeed be greater than the sum of its parts. Use your team!

Self-Talk

Sometimes it is hard to pinpoint the cause of stress. When tangible stress-producing agents cannot be identified, it becomes necessary for teachers to examine how they think and talk to themselves about everyday matters. The way in which individuals talk to themselves can have a significant impact on how they feel about themselves. For example, after failing to meet a targeted goal on time one teacher might think, "Next time I am going to start on the project sooner and not wait till the last minute." Another might say, "I never get things completed on time; I'm just no good." Clearly the first approach provides direction for future actions, while the second labels and condemns the teacher as a failure. Acknowledging the importance of constructive self-talk is a necessary step in realizing the destructiveness of negative self-talk (91).

Positive self-talk can energize the psyche. Teachers should make a point of identifying at least one positive outcome that occurs each day and take credit for that accomplishment. Surely every teacher can think back over the day's events and recall at least one gain or one improvement made by a student, even if it appears to be small or insignificant. Perhaps Sally wrote her name so that it was legible for the first time, Eric gave you distinct eye contact even if it was only for five seconds, or Mark arrived at the resource room on time even if he did not go directly to his seat. Identifying and targeting successes rather than failures is a key to a positive attitude. The way in which teachers think and talk to themselves clearly directs and guides their overt behavior in the classroom.

Research shows that self-talk guides and directs how teachers feel about themselves (92). Learning to talk constructively to yourself about successes and failures can do much to alleviate how you feel and think about stressors in your life. Examples of constructive and destructive self-talk sequences following positive and negative events appear on the next page. Do any of the scenarios sound familiar?

Stroking

Teachers can provide warm strokes to themselves, significant others, and their students. Strokes may be verbal messages, gestures, or tangible objects such as a Fuzzygram (a pleasant narrative that describes an individual's recent accomplishments). They are provided on a contingency basis to others and self after meeting a goal or accomplishing an objective. One thing is certain—teachers feel better about themselves when they give strokes to others—and as a consequence, they frequently receive warm strokes in reciprocation. This creates a wonderfully positive cycle that cannot help but empower special educators to successfully

Positive Event	Constructive Self-Talk
Eric finally succeeds at counting to 25.	At last! That shows if we just keep practicing and practicing, Eric can get it. Next time, when the task seems so impossible, I'm going to remind myself of this success.
	Destructive Self-Talk
	It's about time he got that right. I was about to give up. He really is quite retarded and next time I just won't expect so much. This is really too demanding.

Negative Event	Constructive Self-Talk
Mark loses his temper, knocks over furniture, and swears at the teacher.	Mark is in this class because he has emotional outbursts. Together we are going to restore the environment to its original state and talk about what we can do instead next time when he feels that angry.
	Destructive Self-Talk
	I can't take this anymore. Mark needs to be in a residential treatment center. I just can't control him. I'm no good as a teacher.

combat the stressors they frequently encounter.

Stockpiling a stroke savings account can provide a reservoir of tangible warm strokes that can be drawn from when the going gets rough. Items to be stored for quick retrieval can include notes of appreciation from students or parents, letters of recommendation or commendation or newspaper clippings about the teacher. Special educators can make a withdrawal on their stroke savings account when they are feeling depressed. Reviewing the file can provide a significant lift.

GTMs (Good-to-Myselfs)

These self-given gifts are not connected with any particular performance on the part of the teacher, but are simply reminders that the teacher is a worthy human being and as such deserves as many of the good aspects of life as anyone else. They need not be much—a long, hot soak in the tub, a long-distance telephone call to a friend, a special food—the nurturing gestures that individuals can give to themselves. GTMs are one way to sustain oneself when in need of encouragement that is not forthcoming from other sources.

Remember the Contribution You Are Making

Don't forget why you have chosen to be a special education teacher or a member of a special services staff. Focus on the personal, professional, and philosophical reasons that give meaning to your working hours. Keeping your thoughts on the handicapped students you serve, acknowledging yourself for professional accomplishments, and extending empathy to those whom society often rejects can help you cope with an unsympathetic principal, difficult parents, an inane meeting, or the endless paperwork that passes through your hands. You are a special person because of your willingness and dedication to help others who are less fortunate.

CONCLUSION

As special educators experience stress and burnout, students are affected in turn. Overstressed teachers think only of their own survival in the classroom; the needs of students become secondary. Certainly, yelling at students, overeating, or arriving late to work are unproductive ways of dealing with stress.

It is important to realize that stress among special educators is not a temporary phenomenon that can easily be eradicated through a short-term, cosmetic approach. Teachers must identify for themselves which techniques to include in their personal burnout prevention programs, keeping in mind that each person has a unique conditioning history and that an effective strategy for one person may not yield positive results for another.

A proactive approach of identifying effective stress-reduction strategies is far superior to a retroactive approach of trying to rekindle the fire of a burned-out teacher. While the techniques presented here are not novel, they reflect a wide range of real possibilities for constructively coping with the problem of stress.

7. YOU CAN DO IT

Special education teachers as a whole are a dedicated and caring group of individuals. In a recent study, most of the teachers interviewed said they had always wanted to teach; they had become teachers because they had always wanted to help students learn; and they felt a strong sense of mission (93). For teachers such as these, admitting stress or the onset of burnout may undermine their sense of purpose and self-worth. As a result, they may ignore symptoms and continue the same behavioral patterns, even accelerating the burnout process by attempting to compensate for negative feelings with more work, self-sacrifice, and commitment. These teachers need to sit back, look at what is happening to them, and take a practical approach in establishing a healthy perspective on how they view the workplace. This chapter suggests several ways to do this.

LOCUS OF CONTROL

A personality construct of social learning theory, locus of control refers to a person's perception of whether events are determined internally by his/her own behaviors and ability or externally by fate, luck, or other forces beyond the person's control (94). Researchers have investigated the relationship between the construct and student achievement. A large body of literature has found supportive evidence of a clear-cut relationship between teachers' locus of control and their effectiveness in the classroom (95). For example, there is documentation that classroom behaviors found to be more characteristic of "internal" teachers are those that maximize instructional efficiency. With application to special populations, research suggests that effective special educators are those who perceive themselves as effective change agents in the classroom. That is, they identify influential variables that can facilitate performance and manipulate these variables to bring about desired changes in the students they teach. They do not blame students, parents, or the system for the problems they encounter; instead they take responsibility for resolving the problems themselves.

A *Teacher Locus of Control Scale* is available in the literature (96). It identifies positive and negative events that happen in the classroom and requires the teacher to respond in terms of why the consequence occurred. Following are two examples:

Positive Loaded Item

1. When the grades of your students improve it is more likely

a. because you found ways to motivate the students or

b. because the students were trying harder to do well.

Negative Loaded Item

2. When some of your students fail a math test, it is more likely

a. because you didn't use enough examples to illustrate the concept or

b. because they weren't attending to the lesson.

Clearly, the internal response in both examples is ''a.'' Professionally speaking, in both ''a'' responses the teacher is taking the responsibility for the positive or negative outcome that resulted.

It is crucial that teachers take a high degree of responsibility for the performance of the learners they teach. In the field of special education, it becomes easy to blame failures and lack of progress on the identified disability—that is, the child's label (e.g., John can't read well because he's dyslexic). If special educators do not distinctly see themselves as change agents in the classroom, they can quickly become discouraged by fixating on the variables they cannot control in the handicapped student's environment. This external orientation leads to an outlook of ''learned helplessness''—perceiving oneself as incapable of effecting change in one's environment, even when one can. When this perspective is adopted, ineffective teaching evolves and stress begins to take its toll. Ultimately, the special educator loses professional pride and the rust out or burnout phenomenon ensues.

CULTIVATING STRESS HARDINESS

''No one said teaching was going to be easy, but they didn't tell me it was going to be like this!'' Most teachers in every area of education are familiar with this syndrome. Such expressions usually call to mind a picture of a harried and tired-looking teacher who has had a long day and obviously works many hours beyhond the call of duty. But—HOW LONG WILL THIS TEACHER LAST IN THE FIELD?

The statistics confirm the worst fears—the high number of teachers leaving the profession every year is fact not fiction:

- It is estimated that 50 percent of the members of the teaching profession will leave teaching by 1992 (97).
- In the next 10 years more that 1 million public school teachers, the majority of whom are sincerely dedicated to teaching, will leave the profession in the United States (98).
- Of 9,000 elementary school teachers surveyed regarding health problems associated with teaching, 84 percent indicated there are inherent health hazards (99).

- In a National Education Association opinion poll 60 percent of the respondents did not plan to stay in teaching until retirement (100).
- A survey conducted in Idaho revealed that the attrition rate for special education teachers with one to two years of experience was near 50 percent (101).
- A study conducted in the San Diego school district showed that 90 percent of the educators surveyed reported stress as a common cause of sick leave (102).
- In Chicago, of 5,500 teachers surveyed, 56 percent reported having physical or mental problems as a direct result of their job (103).
- Teacher stress and burnout may cost as much as $3.5 billion annually in absenteeism, turnover, and poor job performance (104).

The average teacher works 50.4 hours each week; the average salary for public school teachers in the United States is less than $23,000 a year (105). Many teachers feel powerless, frustrated, unappreciated—even, as one experienced teacher put it, "set up to experience constant failure" (106, pp. 421-22). But burnout is not an inevitable outcome of high stress. Even though some of the conditions that created stress are beyond the individual teacher's control, it is possible to cope successfully with both the symptoms and the disease itself.

Why do some teachers burn out and others do not? Holt, Fine, and Tollefson conducted a study of elementary teachers who experienced high stress and low burnout and elementary teachers who experienced high stress and high burnout (107). The results clearly indicate that the two groups showed significant differences in their orientations toward life. Teachers in the high-stress/high-burnout group tended to choose passive strategies to cope with stress, such as cutting out activities or becoming angry. Their physical health was poor, with a high incidence of both mental and physical illness. They tended to have an external locus of control—that is, to see themselves as "victims of the changes in their environment" (p. 56). And they experienced higher levels of alienation. Teachers in the high-stress/low-burnout group used active coping strategies, such as getting involved in a hobby or adopting a humorous attitude. They were generally healthier. They had a more internal locus of control, taking a proactive rather than a reactive approach to events in their lives. And they "felt more involved in the various aspects of their life, including work, self, family, interpersonal relationships, and social institutions" (p. 56).

These researchers mentioned three overall factors that seem to contribute to stress hardiness: (1) commitment—"the tendency to be involved in (rather than alienated from) many aspects of one's life"; (2) challenge—"the belief that change, rather than stability, is characteristic of life"; and (3) control—believing and acting "as if one is influential (rather than helpless) in affecting the course of events in one's life'' (pp. 51-52). Cultivating these elements as part of a continuing life plan can serve as stress inoculation.

HOW DO YOU COPE WITH STRESS?

One approach for identifying ways in which special educators are coping with stress that has been successfully used by Dedrick and Raschke is the Q-sort formboard (108). The basis of the Q-sort approach is the notion that all teachers have a perception of the "real situation" and an idealized perception of the way they would like it to be (the "idealized situation"). Discrepancies between these perceptions reflect teachers' dissatisfactions with their profession and may assist them in obtaining a more objective perspective on pinpointing and identifying the real stress elicitors.

Chart 7.1 is a Q-sort formboard designed to help teachers identify variables contributing to their stress in the workplace. The formboard has 16 squares arranged in a stair-step pattern. Below are the labels "Most Like Me," "Very Much Like Me," "A Little Like Me," "Undecided," "A Little Unlike Me," "Very Much Unlike Me," and "Most Unlike Me," numbered 1 through 7. In order to objectify and quantify the ways you are coping with stress, rank the 16 strategies listed ranging from those you perceive as "most like me" to those you perceive as "most unlike me." Add the appropriate number (1–7) to each Q-sort item or write the strategy in the appropriate square of the stair-step pattern.

As will be readily noted, of the 16 choices, eight target a positive orientation for coping with stress and eight target a negative orientation. How did you rank? Are you using strategies that emphasize a positive orientation? Many times teachers are surprised at the results of such a survey. Honesty in responding to the survey and using the information obtained to take an objective look at the situation are key components in learning to cope more effectively with stress.

Positive Orientation	*Negative Orientation*
1. Utilize suport group	1. Overeat
2. Hobbies	2. Confront other staff members
3. Laugh/Humor	3. Leave profession
4. Plan	4. Arrive late
5. Focus on accomplishments	5. Complain to administration
6. Exercise	6. Use punitive measures
7. Read	7. Ventilate frustration
8. Solicit positive comments	8. Yell at students

Chart 7.1
Q-Sort Formboard of Ways the Special Educator Deals with Job-Related Stress

1. Most Like Me	2. Very Much Like Me	3. A Little Like Me	4. Undecided	5. A Little Unlike Me	6. Very Much Unlike Me	7. Most Unlike Me
	Overeat	Arrive late		Ventilate frustration	Confront other staff members	
	Utilize support group	Complain to administration		Read	Leave profession	
	Hobbies	Exercise		Solicit positive comments	Plan	
	Laugh/ Humor	Use punitive measures		Yell at students	Focus on accomplishments	

Teacher Q-Sort Items

HELPING YOURSELF

If you are not satisfied with your stress-coping methods and would like to adopt some alternative strategies, you are encouraged to complete the contract addressing a Stress Reduction Action Plan. (A filled-in sample and a blank contract follow.) The contract requires you to identify sources of the stress, determine ownership for the stressor(s), and pinpoint strategies that you plan to incorporate in an attempt to reduce the stress you are currently experiencing. Problems you own can be tackled directly and, most likely, you will experience more immediate satisfactory results in these instances than with problems you do not own. Nevertheless, a structured formal approach can frequently help the special educator target problems more objectively and establish strategies for improving the situation.

A contract helps the teacher objectify his/her perceptions of ongoing events that are contributing to stress buildup. A plan of action formulated on paper as a permanent product can exemplify a genuine commitment to improve the situation. This tangible indicator of sincerity to positively alter a conflict can, in and of itself, do much to abate stress.

CONCLUSION

Although there are no certain cures for avoiding or dealing with stress, a variety of common strategies available for stress management and burnout prevention have been provided. These strategies have been found helpful by many people.

Unquestionably, the daily lives of special educators are made up of very complex interrelationships for which simple solutions are difficult to find. It is hoped, however, that the strategies presented here will enable these teachers to formulate their own programs of stress management. One good idea in the proper hands can blossom into an elegantly simple yet effective technique. In other cases it will be a difficult task. The challenge is yours. The way in which you think about things, the activities in which you engage, and the support services you solicit make the difference. The benefits that accrue from the effective implementation of stress management techniques in both professional and personal life are well worth the effort.

Stress Reduction Action Plan
(Sample)

Source of Stress: Uncooperative regular educator who mainstreams two students with special needs.

Ownership: Self, regular education teacher, administrator

Evaluation: After four weeks of implementation

	Effectiveness			
Strategies	Excellent	Satisfactory	Poor	Ineffective
1. Talk to the principal to help identify any incentives that can be provided to the regular education teacher.	☐	☐	☐	☐
2. Identify three ways I can provide positive feedback to the regular education teacher for accommodating two students.	☐	☐	☐	☐
3. Design highly motivational program I could implement to help my students perform in the regular education classroom.	☐	☐	☐	☐
4. Reward myself each day I have positive exchange with the regular education teacher.	☐	☐	☐	☐

Evaluation

After one month things are beginning to improve. Both special-needs students want to go to the regular classroom, which is a significant improvement. The regular education teacher speaks to me when we pass in the hallway and is working with the students. While there is much progress yet to be made, a substantial improvement is noted.

Decision

Begin fading motivational program for students. Continue providing positive feedback to regular education teacher. Write a note of appreciation to the principal. Get that cassette tape for myself that I've been working for.

Stress Reduction Action Plan

Source of Stress:
Ownership:
Evaluation:

	Effectiveness			
Strategies	Excellent	Satisfactory	Poor	Ineffective
1.				
	☐	☐	☐	☐
2.				
	☐	☐	☐	☐
3.				
	☐	☐	☐	☐
4.				
	☐	☐	☐	☐

Evaluation

Decision

REFERENCES

Chapter 1. Stress and Burnout, pp. 9–12.

1. Maslach, C., "Burned-out," *Human Behavior* (September 1976): 16–22.
2. Maslach, C., "Understanding Burnout: The Definitional Issues Involved in Analyzing a Complex Phenomenon," in *Job Stress and Burnout*, edited by W. S. Paine (Beverly Hills, Calif.: Sage, 1982): pp. 29–40.
3. Gold, Y. "Recognizing and Coping with Academic Burnout," *Contemporary Education* 59, no. 3 (Spring 1988): 142–45.
4. Blase, J. J., "A Social-Psychological Grounded Theory of Teacher Stress and Burnout," *Educational Administration Quarterly* 18 (1982): 93–113.
5. Holland, R. P., "Special Educator Burnout," *Educational Horizons* (Winter 1982): 58–64.
6. Kaiser, J. S., "Teacher Longevity: Motivation or Burnout," *Clearing House* 56 (September 1982): 17–19.
7. Schwab, R. L. "Teacher Burnout: Moving Beyond 'Psychobabble,' " *Theory into Practice* 22, no. 1 (1984): 21–26.
8. Lortie, D. C., *Schoolteacher: A Sociological Study* (Chicago: University of Chicago Press, 1975).
9. DeShong, B., *The Special Educator: Stress and Survival* (Rockville, Md.: Aspen, 1981).
10. Feistritzer Associates, *The American Teacher* (Washington, D.C.: Feistritzer Associates, 1983).
11. Raschke, D. B.; Dedrick, C. V.; Strathe, M.; and Hawkes, R. R., "Teacher Stress: The Elementary Teacher's Perspective," *Elementary School Journal* 85 (1985): 559–64.
12. Lawrenson, G. M., and McKinnon, A. J., "A Survey of Classroom Teachers of the Emotionally Disturbed: Attrition and Burnout Factors," *Behavior Disorders* 8 (1982): 41–49.
13. Mark, J. H., and Anderson, D. B., "Teacher Survival Rates: A Current Look," *American Educational Research Journal* 15 (1978): 379–83.
14. McGuire, W., "Teacher Burnout," *Today's Education* 68 (November-December 1979): 5.
15. National Education Association, *Teacher Opinion Poll, 1983* (Washington, D.C.: NEA Research Division, 1983).
16. Raschke, D. B.; Dedrick, C. V.; Strathe, M.; and Hawkes, R. R., "Teacher Stress."
17. DeShong, B., *The Special Educator.*
18. Zabel, R. H.; Boomer, L. W.; and King, T. R., "A Model of Stress and Burnout among Teachers of Behaviorally Disordered Students," *Behavior Disorders* 9 (1984): 215–21.
19. Olson, J., and Matuskey, P. V., "Causes of Burnout in SLD Teachers," *Journal of Learning Disabilities* 15 (1982): 97–99.

20. Greer, J. G., and Wethered, C. E., "Learned Helplessness: A Piece of the Burnout Puzzle," *Exceptional Children* 50 (1984): 524–30.

21. Dedrick, C. V., and Raschke, D. B., "Stress and the Special Educator," in *Monograph on Behavior Disorders: Severe Disorders of Children and Youth*, edited by R. B. Rutherford and J. W. Maag, Vol. 11 (Reston, Va.: Council for Children with Behavior Disorders, 1988, pp. 177–87).

22. Fimian, M. J., and Santoro, T. M., "Sources and Manifestations of Occupational Stress as Reported by Full-Time Special Education Teachers," *Exceptional Children* 46 (1983): 540–43.

23. Dixon, B.; Shaw, S. F.; and Bensky, J. M., "Administrator's Role in Fostering the Mental Health of Special Services Personnel," *Exceptional Children* 47, no. 1 (September 1980): 30–36.

24. Dedrick, and Raschke, "Stress and the Special Educator."

Chapter 2. Beware: It Could Happen to You, pp. 13–21.

25. Brodinsky, Ben. "Something Happened to Education in the 1970s," *Phi Delta Kappan* (December 1979).

26. Morris, Sidney, Personal communication to author, 1989.

27. Keogh, B. K., "Learning Disabilities: Diversity in Search of Order," in *The Handbook of Special Education: Research and Practice*, edited by M. C. Wang; M. C. Reynolds; and H. J. Walberg (Oxford, England: Pergamon, in press).

28. Gerber, M. N., "Application of Cognitive Behavioral Training Methods to Teaching Basic Skills to Mildly Handicapped Elementary School Students," in *The Handbook of Special Education: Research and Practice*, edited by M. C. Wang; M. C. Reynolds; and H. J. Walberg (Oxford, England: Pergamon, in press).

29. Neisworth, J. T., and Smith, R. M., *Retardation* (New York: McGraw-Hill, 1978).

30. Reschly, D. J., "Learning Characteristics of Mildly Handicapped Students: Implications for Classification, Placement, and Programming," in *The Handbook of Special Education: Research and Practice*, edited by M. C. Wang; M. C. Reynolds; and H. J. Walberg (Oxford, England: Pergamon, in press).

31. Smith, C. R.; Wood, F. H.; and Grimes, J., "Issues in the Identification and Placement of Behaviorally Disordered Students," in *The Handbook of Special Education: Research and Practice*, edited by M. C. Wang; M. C. Reynolds; and H. J. Walberg (Oxford, England: Pergamon, in press).

32. Nelson, C. M. and Rutherford, R. B., "Behavioral Interventions with Behaviorally Disordered Students," in *The Handbook of Special Education: Research and Practice*, edited by M. C. Wang; M. C. Reynolds; and H. J. Walberg (Oxford, England: Pergamon, in press).

33. Dweck, C. S. and Repucci, N. D., "Learned Helplessness and Reinforcement Responsibility in Children," *Journal of Personality and Social Psychology* 25 (1973): 109–16.

34. Mascari, B. G. and Forgmone, C., "A Follow-up Study of EMR Students

Four Years After Dismissal from the Program," *Education and Training of the Mentally Retarded* 17 (1982): 288–92.

35. Fox, P. B., "Locus of Control and Self-Concept in Mildly Retarded Adolescents," (doctoral dissertation, University of Minnesota, 1972); Dissertation Abstracts International, 1972, 33, 3207B (University Microfilms, No. 72–32, 287).

36. Workman, E., and Hector, M., "Behavior Self-Control in Classroom Settings: A Review of the Literature," *Journal of School Psychology* 16 (1978): 227–36.

Chapter 3. The Impact of Stress on Teachers, Students, and Organizational Components, pp. 22–30.

37. Selye, H., *Stress without Distress* (Philadelphia: Lippincott, 1974).

38. Selye, H., *The Stress of Life* (New York: McGraw-Hill, 1976).

39. Epanchin, B. C., and Paul, J. L., *Casebook for Educating the Emotionally Disturbed* (Columbus, Ohio: Charles E. Merrill, 1982).

40. Kounin, J., *Discipline and Group Management in Classrooms* (New York: Holt, Rinehart and Winston, 1970).

41. Deal, T. E., "The Culture of Schools," in *Leadership: Examining the Elusive*, edited by Linda T. Sheive and Marian B. Schoenheit (Alexandria, Va.; Association for Supervision and Curriculum Development, 1987).

42. Conley, S. C.; Schmidle, J.; and Shedd, J. B., "Teacher Participation in the Management of School Systems," *Teachers College Record* 90 (1988): 259–80.

43. Gordon, T., *Teacher Effectiveness Training* (New York: David McKay, 1974).

44. Raschke, D. B.; Dedrick, C. V.; and DeVries, A., "Coping with Stress: The Special Educator's Perspective," *Teaching Exceptional Children* 21 (Fall 1988): 10–14.

45. Polloway, E. A., "Identification and Placement in Mild Mental Retardation Programs: Recommendations for Professional Practice," *Education and Training of the Mentally Retarded* 20 (1985): 218–21.

46. Stainback, S., and Stainback, W., *Integration of Students with Severe Handicaps into Regular Schools* (Reston, Va.: Council for Exceptional Children, 1985).

Chapter 4. Stress and the Special Educator, pp. 31–50.

47. Schwab, R. L., and Iwanicki, E. F., "Who Are Our Burned-out Teachers?" *Educational Research Quarterly* 17, no. 2 (Summer 1982).

48. D'Alonzo, B. J., and Wiseman, D. E., "Actual and Desired Roles of the High School Learning Disability Resource Teacher," *Journal of Learning Disabilities* 11 (June/July 1978): 390–97.

49. Zabel, R. H.; Boomer, L. W.; and King, T. R., "A Model of Stress and Burnout among Teachers of Behaviorally Disordered Students," *Behavior Disorders* 9 (1984): 215–21.

50. Rizzo, J. R.; House, R. J.; and Lirtzman, S. I., "Role Conflict and Ambiguity in Complex Organizations," *Administration Sciences Quarterly* 15 (1970): 150–63.

51. Lawrenson G. M., and McKinnon, A. J. "A Survey of Classroom Teachers of the Emotionally Disturbed: Attrition and Burnout Factors," *Behavior Disorders* 8 (1982): 41–49.

52. Fimian M. J., and Santoro, T. M. "Sources and Manifestations of Occupational Stress as Reported by Full-Time Special Education Teachers," *Exceptional Children* 46 (1983): 540–43.

53. Bradfield, R. H., and Fones, D. M., "'Stress and the Special Teacher: How Bad Is It?" *Academic Therapy* 20 (May 1985): 571–77.

54. D'Alonzo and Wiseman, "Actual and Desired Roles."

55. Morsink, C. V.; Blackhurst, A. E.; and Williams, S., "SOS: Follow-up Support to Beginning Learning Disabilities Teachers," *Journal of Learning Disabilities* 12, no. 3 (March 1979): 17–21.

56. Bensky, J. M.; Shaw, S. F.; Gouse, A. S.; Bates, H.; Dixon, B.; and Beane, W. E., "Public Law 94-142 and Stress: A Problem for Educators," *Exceptional Children* 47, no. 1 (September 1980): 24–29.

57. Olson, J., and Matuskey, P. V., "Causes of Burnout in SLD Teachers," *Journal of Learning Disabilities* 15 (1982): 97–99.

58. Fimian, M. J.; Pierson, D.; and McHardy R., "Occupational Stress Reported by Teachers of Learning Disabled and Nonlearning Disabled Handicapped Students," *Journal of Learning Disabilities* 19 (1986): 154–58.

59. Johnson, A. B.; Gold, V.; and Vickers, L. L., "Stress and Teachers of the Learning Disabled, Behavior Disordered, and Educable Mentally Retarded," *Psychology in the Schools* 19 (October 1982): 552–57.

60. Zabel, Boomer, and King, "A Model of Stress and Burnout."

61. Jones, R. L., "Morale of Teachers of Mentally Retarded Children: An Exploratory Investigation," *Education and Training of the Mentally Retarded* 4, no. 1 (February 1969): 4–10.

Chapter 5. Organizational/Personal Strategies for Coping with Stress, pp. 51–57.

62. Minner, S., and Beane, A., "Q-Sorts for Special Education Teachers," *Teaching Exceptional Children* 11 (1985): 279–81.

63. Raschke, D. B.; Dedrick, C. V.; Strathe, M.; and Hawkes, R. R., "Teacher Stress: The Elementary Teacher's Perspective," *Elementary School Journal* 85 (1985): 559–64.

64. Johnson, A. B.; Gold, V.; and Vickers, L. I., "Stress and Teachers of Learning Disabled, Behavior Disordered, and Educable Mentally Retarded," *Psychology in the Schools* 19 (October 1982): 552–57.

65. Dunham, J., "Disruptive Pupils and Teacher Stress," *Educational Researcher* 23, no. 3 (June 1981): 205–13.

66. Schwab, R. L.; Jackson, S. E.; and Schuler, R. S., "Educator Burnout:

Sources and Consequences," *Educational Research Quarterly* 10 (1986): 14–29.

67. Weiskopf, P. E., "Burnout Among Teachers of Exceptional Children," *Exceptional Children* 47, no. 1 (September 1980): 18–23.
68. Holt, P.; Fine, M. J.; and Tollefson, N., "Mediating Stress: Survival of the Hardy," *Psychology in the Schools* 24 (1987): 51–58.
69. Gold, Y. "Recognizing and Coping with Academic Burnout," *Contemporary Education* 59, no. 3 (Spring 1988): 143–45.

Chapter 6. Preventive and Remedial Strategies for Coping with Stress, pp. 58–73.

70. Fredericks, B., *A Data-Based Classroom for the Moderately and Mildly Handicapped* (Monmouth, Ore.: Instructional Development Corporation, 1975).
71. Pearson, D., and Shaw, S. *Life Extension: A Practical Approach* (New York: Warner Books, 1982).
72. Rapp, D. J., "Food Allergy Treatment for Hyperkinesis," *Journal of Learning Disabilities* 12 (1979); 42–50.
73. Marlatt, C. A.; Pagano, R. R.; Rose, R. M.; and Marques, J. K., "Effects of Meditation and Relaxation Training upon Alcohol Use in Male Social Drinkers," in *Meditation: Classic and Contemporary Perspectives*, edited by D. H. Shapiro and R. N. Walsh (New York: Aldine, 1984).
74. Quick, J. C., and Quick, J. D., *Organizational Stress and Preventive Management* (New York: McGraw-Hill, 1984).
75. Smith, J. C., and Siebert, J. R., "Self-Reported Physical Stress Reactions: First- and Second-Order Factors," *Biofeedback and Self-Regulation* 9 (1984): 215–27.
76. Engel, B. T.; Glasgow, M. S.; and Gaarder, K. R., "Behavioral Treatment of High Blood Pressure III: Follow-up Results and Treatment Recommendations," *Psychosomatic Medicine* 45 (1983): 23–39.
77. Parks, A. L., and Fairchild, T. N., *How to Survive Educator Burnout* (Dayton, Ohio: Kids Come in Special Flavors Co., 1981).
78. Shapiro, D. H., and Walsh, R. N., eds., *Meditation: Classic and Contemporary Perspectives* (New York: Aldine, 1984).
79. Beiman, I.; Israel, E.; and Johnson, S. A., "Training and Posttraining Effects of Live and Taped Extended Progressive Relaxation, Self-Relaxation, and Electromyogram Biofeedback," *Journal of Consulting and Clinical Psychology* 46 (1978): 314–21.
80. Tubesing, N. L., and Tubesing, D. A., eds., *Structured Exercises in Stress Management*, Vol. I (Duluth, Minn.: Whole Person Press, 1983).
81. Tubesing, N. L., and Tubesing, D. A., eds., *Structured Exercises in Stress Management*, Vol. II (Duluth, Minn.: Whole Person Press, 1984).
82. Tubesing, N. L., and Tubesing, D. A., eds., *Structured Exercises in Stress Management*, Vol. III (Duluth, Minn.: Whole Person Press, 1986).

83. Cautela, J. R., and Groden, J., *Relaxation: A Comprehensive Manual for Adults, Children and Children with Special Needs* (Champaign, Ill.: Research Press, 1978).
84. Quick, J. C., and Quick, J. D., *Organizational Stress.*
85. Ibid.
86. Puente, A. E., and Beiman, I., "The Effects of Behavior Therapy, Self-Relaxation, and Transcendental Meditation and Cardiovascular Stress Response," *Journal of Clinical Psychology* 36 (1980): 291–95.
87. Sisley, T., "Timely Tips: Time Management for the Administration," *Physical Educator* 40 (1983): 75–77.
88. Cohen, S. B., and Hart-Hester, S., "Time Management Strategies," *Teaching Exceptional Children* 20 (1987): 56–57.
89. Bergman, M., "Networking: How to Build a Support System," *Choices* 3 (1986): 11–13.
90. Taylor, L., and Salend, S. J., "Reducing Stress-Related Burnout Throughout a Network Support System," *Pointer* 27 (1983): 5–9.
91. Meichenbaum, D. H., *Cognitive Behavior Modification: An Integrative Approach* (New York: Plenum Press, 1977).
92. Kendall, P., "On the Efficacious Use of Verbal Self-Instruction Procedures with Children," *Cognitive Therapy and Research* 1 (1977): 331–41.

Chapter 7. You Can Do It, pp. 74–81.

93. McLaughlin, M. W.; Pfeifer, R. S.; Swanson-Owens, D.; and Yee, S., "Why Teachers Won't Teach," *Phi Delta Kappan* 67, no. 6 (1986): 420–26.
94. Rotter, J. B., *Social Learning and Clinical Psychology* (New York: Prentice-Hall, 1954).
95. Lefcourt, H. M., *Locus of Control: Current Trends in Therapy and Research*, 2d ed. (Hillside, N.J.: Erlbaum, 1982).
96. Rose, J. S., and Medway, F. J., "Measurement of Teachers' Belief in Their Control over Student Outcome," *Journal of Educational Research* 74 (1981): 185–90.
97. Carnegie Forum on Education and the Economy, *A Nation Prepared: Teachers for the 21st Century* (Washington, D.C.: the Forum, Task Force on Teaching as a Profession, 1986).
98. McLaughlin, Pfeifer, Swanson-Owens, and Yee, "Why Teachers Won't Teach."
99. Rosenthal, E.; Harlin, V. K.; and Jerrick, S. J., "Is Teaching Hazardous to Your Health?" *Instructor* 86 (1976): 55–58.
100. McGuire, W., "Teacher Burnout," *Today's Education* 68 (November December 1979): 5.
101. Truch, S., *Teacher Burnout and What to Do About It* (Novato, Calif.: Academic Therapy Publications, 1980).
102. Parks, A. L., and Fairchild, T. N., *How to Survive Educator Burnout* (Dayton, Ohio: Kids Come in Special Flavors Co., 1981).

103. Walsh, D., "Classroom Stress and Teacher Burnout," *Phi Delta Kappan* 61 (1979): 253.
104. Truch, *Teacher Burnout*.
105. "Teachers Work Long Hours for Low Pay," Center for Statistics, *Phi Delta Kappan* 68, no. 5 (1987): 408.
106. McLaughlin, Pfeifer, Swanson-Owens, and Yee, "Why Teachers Won't Teach."
107. Holt, P.; Fine, M. J.; and Tollefson, N. "Mediating Stress: Survival of the Hardy." *Psychology in the Schools* 24 (1987): 51–58.
108. Dedrick, C.V., and Raschke, D. B., "Stress and the Special Educator," in *Monograph on Behavior Disorders: Severe Disorders of Children and Youth*, edited by R. B. Rutherford and J. W. Maag, Vol. 11 (Reston, Va.: Council for Children with Behavior Disorders, 1988, pp. 177–87).